What early readers a
ONE BRICK A

"I was mesmerized reading Rich Walton's book about his intriguing and mind-boggling adventures in Afghanistan. If you are up for a wild, first-hand account of what it's like to conduct business in a frenzied, war-torn setting, make sure you pick up a copy of *One Brick at a Time*."

—Greg Jacob, professor, author and Fulbright Scholar

"*One Brick at a Time* depicts what it takes to succeed in life and business. Mr. Rich's adventures provide lessons in networking and just 'how to get things done.' This entertaining story of a businessman's experience in a combat war zone will engage all types of readers"

—Troy Kenning, Lt. Colonel, USAF, Afghanistan Veteran

"A fascinating account ...Rich Walton brings you incredible first-hand experiences of amazing true stories of his journeys throughout Afghanistan. *One Brick at a Time* is a riveting story and a great read."
—Doug Bomarito, JD, USNA 1968, U.S. Navy Vietnam Combat Veteran

"Rich and I met in front of the Safi hotel in downtown Kabul in 2009. We were fellow Naval Academy parents both working 'outside the wire' in Afghanistan. Reading his account took me back to the sights and sounds of living in a country at war but also learning to understand a culture so different from our own. There are roses in Afghanistan but as the Afghan saying goes, 'there is no rose without the thorn.' I highly recommend reading this to get the rest of the story usually not told."

—Elaine Brye, Military Mom of 4, Teacher at International School of Kabul, author, *Be Safe, Love Mom*

"Rich Walton's in-depth analysis of what really goes on within Afghanistan is mind boggling. While our troops were in Afghanistan, they lived on-base, and except for minor encounters with the Taliban, they were separated from the Afghans. On the other hand, Rich Walton worked hand-in-hand with the Afghans the entire time he was in the country. He learned facts about the country of Afghanistan at the worker level. His book describes Afghanistan at the street level. After all that was said during our withdrawal, Rich's book tells it as it is. It is a must read."

—CAPT Tim Myers, USNA 1964, US Navy (Retired)

"In view of current world events and especially with what is currently happening in South Asia, Rich Walton's experiences in Afghanistan are very interesting and timely. In this book, *One Brick at a Time*, Rich details the trials and rewards of being an American contractor in a historically tribal nation in a modern world!"

—Raymond A. Kutch, USNA 1963, Former Flight Officer, Vietnam Veteran

ONE BRICK AT A TIME

WINNING HEARTS & MINDS IN AFGHANISTAN

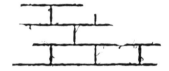

Rich Walton

PRESS

Portland, Oregon

One Brick at a Time Press
15900 NW Gillihan Road
Portland, OR 97231

www.OneBrickataTimePress.com

This is a work of actual experiences. Some names of characters have been changed as of the author's imagination to protect identities. Any similarity to actual persons' names, living or dead, is completely coincidental

Cover Design - SSG. Jeffrey T. Walton, US Army
　　　　Anita Jones anotherjones.com

Interior Design - Anita Jones anotherjones.com

All photos were taken by Rich Walton unless otherwise noted.

ISBN 978-1-7378588-0-5 print
ISBN 978-1-7378588-1-2 ebook

Publisher's Cataloging-In-Publication Data
(Prepared by The Donohue Group, Inc.)

Names: Walton, Rich, 1951- author.
Title: One brick at a time : winning hearts & minds in Afghanistan / Rich Walton.
Description: Portland, Oregon : One Brick at a Time Press, [2022] | Includes bibliographical references and index.
Identifiers: ISBN 9781737858805 (print) | ISBN 9781737858812 (ebook)
Subjects: LCSH: Walton, Rich, 1951- | Businesspeople--United States--Biography. | Government contractors--United States--Biography. | Construction industry--Afghanistan. | Success in business. | LCGFT: Autobiographies.
Classification: LCC HC102.5.W349 A3 2022 (print) | LCC HC102.5.W349 (ebook) | DDC 338.092--dc23

Printed in the United States for America

Dedication

To my wife, Shirley and our sons, Richard, Jeff & Tommy,
who encouraged me with unwavering support to go live
these adventures.

To all the U.S. military servicemen and women and civilian
contractors I served with in Iraq and Afghanistan, to whom
my life was entrusted for protection.

And to the Afghan people whom I was able to share
four years of my life.

The memory of those I served with at FOB Smart,
the ones who came home and those that did not.

Acknowledgments

I would like to acknowledge all the people I served with in Iraq and Afghanistan who were in service of our country.

I am fortunate that my Mom and Dad always encouraged my brother, sisters and me to be adventurous and go live our dreams.

I want to thank my wife Shirley for her endless support and encouragement, allowing me to deploy and live the experiences and adventures you'll read about in this book and my sons, Richard, Jeff & Tommy for their support and helping their mother hold down the home front. When I was deployed, it was not only a hardship on me but just as much or more a hardship on my wife and family.

I also thank Major Jim Ellis Retired US Army, for encouraging me to go to Afghanistan, saying it would be a great adventure & experience. He was right.

Writing this book was a huge struggle for me. It was much easier for me to live the stories than to write about them. I thank Rachel Lulich for her countless hours of editing and guiding, plus Amanda Clarke for her colorful descriptive help. And thank our son, Jeff Walton for tirelessly designing the cover over and over again and Shirley, how many times did you read this to me to fix, change and correct.

A special thanks to Sharon Castlen, Integrated Book Marketing, for being so excited about marketing my book.

I am grateful for all the Afghan people I had the privilege of meeting and sharing cups of tea.

And I thank God for the opening and closing of doors as needed for my personal growth, for giving me the nine lives of a cat and for bringing me through these four years unscathed, as my wife says "Prayer and God's protective hands were forever around me."

Special Note From The Author

After 4 ½ years in Afghanistan working to build a better life and environment for the Afghan people, I came home with a burning desire to tell my family and friends what I had experienced and what the Afghan people are like from my point of view as a civilian contractor. Even in a War Zone, what I had learned to appreciate being with the Afghan people was kindness, helpfulness and friendships. The immense complexities of the war that had been going on for so many years was nothing I understood living in isolation and the safety of my home in America.

This book was ready to go to publication in August of 2021 with a different title. Just like the weather changing from a clear day to a horrific sand storm, the recent events of the Taliban came swooping in with no respect of anyone or anything in its path. Mayhem, destruction and death, it is leaving no one untouched.

In the days following the Taliban take over, many people contacted me wanting to know my thoughts on the turn of events in Afghanistan. I was told by Afghans I worked with that the Taliban are like a dog with rabies, that no matter what, there is nothing you can to do to save them. The only solution is to put them down. Afghanistan is a tribal society and the will of many of the Afghan soldiers in my opinion was not dying for a government they didn't understand. There are many Afghan Special forces I met who are awesome fighters and some died fighting the Taliban. But to just leave them on their own was giving those remaining a death sentence.

Because of America being in Afghanistan the last 20 years, the women and girls of Afghanistan have had the freedom to go to school, work outside the home, have jobs in government and careers such as beauticians and basically have been able to choose a life for themselves. This will all be taken away from them.

After this turn of events in August of 2021 in Afghanistan, I believe my book can help the American people better understand the Afghan people and their culture and how far they had come in just 20 years.

One of the things that hit me hard during this turn of events, is all the US military bases that had been named after fallen soldiers in Afghanistan. Most have memorial plaques dedicated to the fallen soldier(s) at each of these bases that sadly will now most likely be destroyed.

For a list of many memorial bases I visited – their names and photos, go to A Few Military Bases with Memorials in Afghanistan at the end of this book.

In addition, because of these recent events, I had to block out people's eyes and faces of my pictures I am sharing with you in this book. I am so sorry you cannot see their expressions of joy and happiness...just having a job.

Looking back I feel blessed to have had the opportunity to live and learn from my experiences in Afghanistan and the Afghan people.

My hope and prayers go out to the Afghan people.

God speed and stay safe.

Richard T. Walton

Contents

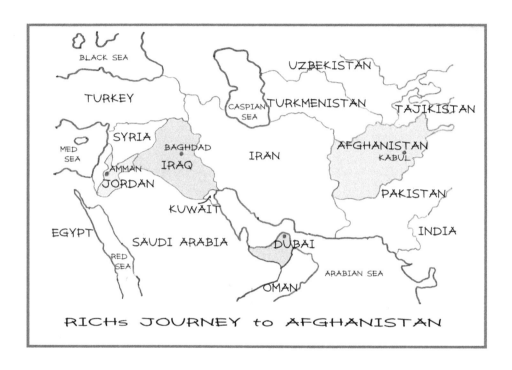

RICHs JOURNEY to AFGHANISTAN

CHAPTER 1

From Construction Zone to War Zone

"Twenty years from now you will be more disappointed by the things you didn't do than by the ones you did do."
—Mark Twain

The plane circled down so fast and shook so violently, I thought it might break in two. It was my first time flying into Baghdad, and I was experiencing the spiral descent pilots made to avoid rockets as they came in for a landing. 48 hours earlier, I had been home in Oregon with my wife Shirley, waiting to find out if I'd gotten a new job as a construction manager in Afghanistan. It was the height of the recession.

For over 30 years, I had built a thriving architectural design firm based in the Pacific Northwest, having a reputation for turning my clients' personal home dreams into reality. Business was good. Then, in 2008 the housing market suddenly crashed, and in came the decline of the real estate market and the home-building depression. The builders I worked with were downsizing or filing for bankruptcy. Needless to say, my business was hit hard financially and the future did not look good.

Looking back, I had become dissatisfied with my day-to-day business routine even before the market crashed. 30 years of sitting at my drawing table, designing new homes and buildings, answering the constant demands of clients who often didn't even know what they wanted, stating; "I don't know what I want, but I will know it when I see it," had made me restless. I remember saying to my wife many times; "I feel like I have to keep re-inventing the wheel every day, is this all I'm ever going to do?" Yet, I really couldn't think of doing any other kind of work that would support our family.

If someone would have told me at the time that I would be spending the next four years in war-torn Afghanistan, I would have told them they were crazy. I never thought that my future would take me half-way around the world into the Middle East, I never dreamed the consequences would have such a major impact on how I viewed the world.

Adding to the challenging upcoming four years' journey to the Middle East was the fact I would end up changing employers every 12-18 months while I was over there, switching back and forth between a civilian contracting company, the U.S. Government and military units.

There have been several thousands of American civilians deployed to Afghanistan and Iraq. Each one has his or her own story of unique experiences to tell. This is mine.

OPPORTUNITY KNOCKS

It has often been said that when one door closes, another door opens. I had never given that saying much thought, much less thought it would apply to me in any way that mattered. But as I struggled to find architectural design work during the recession, opportunity knocked. A friend in Annapolis, Maryland said she had a friend that had a construction business in Iraq. We conveyed to him what I did and that I was willing to travel. After initial small talk, we found out that while he did not have an immediate need for an architectural designer, he did have a pressing need for a construction manager at a new business unit in Afghanistan, which would require me to work in-country. A week later my wife and I jumped on a plane and flew to Annapolis to meet the business owner to talk about his overseas plans.

I knew Afghanistan was the home of the Taliban and would be dangerous, but, with less and less work coming in, I was in panic mode, starting to get desperate for a steady income. I decided to go for it.

Fortunately, I had the skills that met the requirements he needed for this Country Manager job; operating my own business, structural design skills, working with building material suppliers, thinking outside the box for creative and unique problem solving, business networking skills to make things happen and the most important requirement, the ability to function independently.

While several of these items would not be job requirements for a stateside job, the skills package I brought to the table fit the president of the company's vision of what would be needed to be their country manager in Afghanistan. I was knowledgeable of the history of the region, and told him I wanted to be part of history in the making, which probably sealed the deal in my favor for being selected for the job.

Perhaps one of the most important factors in hiring me was the relationship my wife and I had. We had been married over 30 years and our children were grown and in the military, so we knew the risks. The president, appeared a happily married man with children, was a former Army Airborne Ranger, was about six feet tall, wirily slim-built with broad shoulders and a friendly smile, had dark sparkly eyes full of exciting life, a close-cut black beard outlining his square jawline that matched his short bushy dark hair. After a strong solid handshake, he told us he found that many married men were not good candidates for these lengthy overseas assignments because of marital difficulties that might ensue. It was important that my wife accompany me for the interview; she was being interviewed as well. His main question to my wife was if she was ok with her husband going to Afghanistan. She had to be comfortable with me going to a war zone and for great lengths at a time.

The man said if I was serious, I had to formally apply for the job online, and take a few online courses required for those wanting to work in a war zone area overseas. This job required a secret clearance, so I would also have to complete a lengthy security clearance application. My wife and I flew back to Portland and because my architectural work was diminishing, we wondered if this deal was real.

During the next 10 days, I filled out the application online, completed the required online courses, went to a medical travel clinic in Portland to get the required vaccinations and Malaria pills for Afghanistan, and with Shirley's help, worked through one full day and all night completing the Security Clearance Application, having to pull dates and information and people from my whole life. I also worked on completing a few architectural business jobs so I could close my business down in a hurry if I actually got the Country Manager position.

When family members found out I was possibly going to Afghanistan to work, at least one of them asked my wife what she and I were thinking. "I wouldn't go there," he said. "Why doesn't Rich stay here in Oregon and go broke like the rest of us?" Needless to say, we did not cave in to the pressure. Rolling over and going broke was not in my game plan. We turned and walked away from comments like that, as we both thought of this as the next adventure.

Almost 2 weeks later, I felt like I was in limbo, not hearing from anyone. I still was not sure anything was going to happen when out of the blue – no phone call, no communication – I got an email from the company with a one way plane ticket to Baghdad attached, telling me I had the job and was to leave for Afghanistan in 48 hours.

ALL HELL BREAKS LOOSE

The following 48 hours were nothing but one big blur.

While finishing closing my business, the email included instructions to buy several articles of sturdy clothing with no noticeable lettering indicating I was an American or drawing attention. I also had to get boots, a backpack and a sleeping bag. I didn't even have time to think. Our Navy son came home for a couple days to help. "You need light brown boots, Dad, the dust will make black boots look dirty all the time." He taught me how to stuff socks and small items in my extra pair of packed boots to get more in my bag.

I was in a whirlwind from the time I received the email until I was going through security at the Portland International Airport to begin my journey.

Standing at the departure gate, I fought back a few rather disturbing fears and butterflies. I have never been in the military and had no idea what I was getting myself into. Plus, I would be traveling alone. I was getting ready to board the first of a series of flights that would end up in Kabul, Afghanistan. The geographical distance from Portland, Oregon to Afghanistan is a mere 7,000 miles, give or take, but the mental travel might as well be measured in light years.

Oh well, I thought, how bad can it get? Lots of guys have done this and survived…right? And I did need the security of the job. Right? Yes, I did.

All I had to do was change planes in Atlanta to get on a flight straight to Dubai and beyond. I kissed my wife goodbye and walked away from everything I knew.

According to the emails I had received, I would have to find the hotel the company had reserved for me for the night in Dubai on my own, and then fly to Baghdad, Iraq in the morning for a two week Middle East orientation at our company headquarters before continuing on to Afghanistan, my final destination.

I was on my way with a one-way ticket to Afghanistan, $300 in my pocket and no contract signed. I had received no money up front and almost no solid information about the construction company beyond what I was told during the job interview.

I felt a little foolish and quite naïve. It all happened so fast, I simply took the job on faith and had no clear idea of what I would be doing. Instead of being provided with a job description, I was told "you'll figure it out when you get to Afghanistan." I didn't know anyone over there, and all I knew about Afghanistan was what I had seen on newscasts and read in the paper. I had seen battlefield footage of the Taliban, but right now all I remembered was the sound of incoming mortar rounds in the background as the reporter read the news. I began to panic.

As soon as I arrived in Atlanta, I made a frenzied call to my wife. "Shirley, what am I doing?" I stammered.

"Just go, Rich," she said, very serious but reassuring. "If you don't like it, come home."

How could she be so calm? Our lives were being turned inside out. I was so glad she was the pillar of strength I needed right then. She told me later that seeing me dying at my desk in boredom had made her realize how badly I needed a big change. I got on the plane. A big change is one thing, a death-defying journey into a war zone is quite another.

THE JOURNEY BEGINS

I arrived in Dubai in the morning, after flying all night from Atlanta. I found myself surrounded in an international crowd—a sea of men wearing long white sheet like robes covering them from head to toe. The only variation was the color of men's headdresses draped on their heads like lightweight cotton dish towels; either white, or red plaid, held in place by a black band matching their close-cut black beards. Women were dressed even more conservatively, wearing black hijabs; floor length black sheets, covering their bodies and faces to hide everything. Some eyes showed and some were completely hidden, completely covering everything. It was a stark difference to the dress code of American citizens.

I scanned across the crowd, looking for familiar western faces, wondering how to get to the hotel. Among the ocean of mostly white robes, it was a refreshing sight to see American Private Security Detail (PSD) guys all over the place. I recognized them because of their clothes; typical black t-shirts stretched tight over their bulked-up straight-out-of-the-gym body builder muscles, khaki pants and hiking boots. I just started talking to some American

Private Security Contractors and actually found one of them going to the same hotel I was. I'm sure I looked like a fish out of water, as he took me under his wing out of sympathy.

Dubai came on like a ton of bricks so I had no time for any sense of jet lag. It was almost surreal as I took in the splendor of that magnificent city as the PSD guy and I made our way to the hotel. I was overwhelmed by the spectacle.

Dubai has all the audacious glitter and western decadence of the Las Vegas Strip, worlds apart from where I was heading. Piles of money and luxurious construction seemed to be everywhere I looked. The largest shopping mall in the world.... The tallest building in the world.... Spectacular night clubs everywhere.... I had arrived in the ultimate world of magnificent architecture. But that would all disappear the next day when I returned to the airport to continue my eastward journey.

The dream world that was Dubai faded quickly the next morning as reality sank in on the concourse. The PSD guy told me that it was everyone for themselves to get on the plane for Baghdad. Merely having a ticket did not ensure you would get a seat on the plane. I was flying on Jupiter Airlines. I had never heard of that airline before. There were no assigned seats and no listening for boarding calls over the P.A. system.

I stood at the gate with my fellow travelers in front of the sliding glass doors, like a Black Friday sale with everyone crammed together watching for the doors to electronically open. Once the doors opened, there came a mad dash with everyone pushing, shoving and elbowing to get a seat on the plane.

Being new, I was not aggressive enough to hold my own amidst the chaos, but my American private security friend saved me a seat. The aircraft was an older jet with only one class of seating. There were no snacks. The stench of body odor reminded me of my old football locker room.

In the air and on the approach to Baghdad International, I noticed the young female flight attendant strapping herself in and looking quite nervous. I asked her if everything was OK.

She replied, "Sir, have you never flown into Baghdad before?"

"No, first time," I grinned.

As she warned me to get ready for the spiral descent the plane made to avoid rockets, the jet made a hard right turn.

"Rockets?"

The plane circled down so fast and shook so violently, I thought it might break in two. I quickly realized why they did not serve food on the flight. I could hear people behind me getting sick and smell them throwing up. Right when I was sure we were going to crash, the plane leveled out and landed. I found out later that frequent visitors to the city referred to this spiral descent as a corkscrew landing. It seemed like an appropriate name for this unique runway approach.

I had made it to Baghdad. Now what?

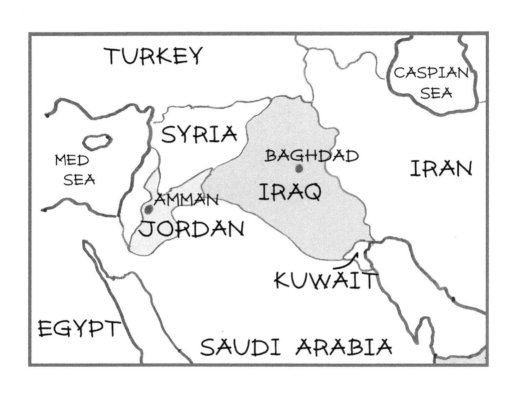

CHAPTER 2

Baghdad

"All life is a chance. So take it! The person who goes the farthest is the one who is willing to do and dare."

—Dale Carnegie

Safely off the Jupiter flight to Baghdad, I thought it a little strange that the aircraft did not taxi, but came to a stop about 1/8 mile from the gate. We had to board a bus to take us the rest of the way to the gate of the terminal. In response to the quizzical look on my face, one of my fellow travelers explained, "If one of these big jets gets blasted by rockets, they don't want it taking out the whole terminal at the same time. You know, the two-for-the-price-of-one!" Between the corkscrew landing and parking so far from the terminal gate, I started wondering what was I getting myself into?

VISA NO GOOD!

Baghdad was a total cultural shock. While going through customs, a uniformed Iraqi carrying an assault rifle pulled me aside and separated me from the American PSD guy and the rest of the passengers. Scrutinizing my passport, the Iraqi yelled in broken English, "Visa no good!" I was abruptly ushered into a back room with him still grasping my passport, my only ticket to freedom. Now I was freaking out. I had heard stories about not giving up your passport, but what was I to do?

After a few minutes of mumbling to each other, one of the uniformed guards yelled at me, "Visa no good, you need to step outside of room and wait!" An eternity passed while I waited on a bench in the hall by myself. Finally, a half hour later, I was called back into the room, where I was angrily told I had to pay more money for a new visa. I nervously handed some money to a gruff looking guy. They took $150, half of what I had. In a bizarre way, he reminded me of the Soup Nazi on the TV show *Seinfeld*, but this was certainly no comedy.

Payoff complete, I was allowed to make my way to baggage claim. I have never been so relieved as when I spotted a guy there holding a sign with my name on it, but my euphoria was short-lived as someone pulled me aside to a special area to have my head scanned checking for Swine Flu. Finally feeling safe back with the man that had my name, I was handed a bullet proof vest to put on.

I thought to myself, "Wow! What is this and how does it fit and strap together?" In spite of my obvious nervousness, he helped me put it on. All of my security looked like body builders. They had short hair and equally short, cropped beards with sunglasses on. Like the American Security Detail, they too wore hiking boots, but had on tan colored pants to match the bullet-proof vests covering up most of the dark T-shirts they wore underneath.

My escorts drove out of the airport like they were in a NASCAR race. I say escorts – plural – because there were three vehicles in my entourage, not one. They seated me in the middle vehicle. My stomach was just getting settled from the turbulent landing and the customs incident, and now I felt like I was in the middle of a high speed chase on a LA freeway. The drivers were weaving in and out of traffic at warp speed, and even crossing over into the oncoming traffic. These guys had no fear.

As I was tossed side to side in the back seat like a ping-pong ball, I managed to ask why we were driving so fast. The driver's explanation that it was because of snipers and roadside bombs almost threw me into a panic attack.

"Roadside bombs?" I stammered.

"Yeah, ya know, IEDs." (Improvised Explosive Device)

Knowing that acronym gave me no comfort whatsoever. The ride from the airport was one of the most memorable of my life. You'll hear me say many times in the upcoming stories that many of my experiences were like being in the movies.

The three-vehicle convoy navigated the crowded city streets, thwarting any armed assailants who might be trying to disrupt our movement. At each intersection, in leapfrog fashion the lead vehicle would stop and everyone would hop out. Toting their AK- 47s, they stopped traffic and let the rear vehicle blast through the intersection with my vehicle in tow. As we cleared the intersection, the stopped vehicle would accelerate to bring up the rear. This maneuver continued as we transversed the city.

I was overwhelmed by my own apparent importance. Did these guys realize I was only the country construction manager for my company, not the President of the United States?

THE GREEN AND RED ZONES

We passed many military vehicles and convoys on the road, but I quickly learned that protecting us civilian contractors was not generally part of the U.S. military's job description.

We were on our own, except for our Personal Security Guards. Our PSD guys carried AK-47 rifles and machine guns, giving me a sense of security in spite of the implication of serious danger. I was relieved to have body guards. I found out quickly that virtually all U.S. and European contractors in dangerous Middle East areas had to have security to protect against attacks and kidnapping. While the military supplied armored vehicles and soldiers for transporting U.S. Government employees around, civilian contractors like me had to depend on body guards our company provided, especially when we ventured outside the protective walls of the bases.

Our entourage finally arrived at which was to be my home for the next couple weeks before moving on to Afghanistan. While in Baghdad, I would get acclimated to the Middle East and obtain a DoD (Department of Defense) badge, needed to gain entry to US bases and government facilities in Afghanistan.

The Green Zone, later called the International Zone, was a fortress compound in the center of Baghdad. Saddam Hussein had turned the riverfront property into a gated city, with posh villas, bungalows, government buildings, shops, and even a hospital. With the American influence coming into Baghdad, the Green Zone was equipped with all the comforts of home – sort of – including a Burger King and Dairy Queen. It had morphed into "Little America" in the heart of Baghdad, where people jogged in the streets. A surreal environment in the middle of a war zone.

Downtown Baghdad Statue

Unfortunately, since I was a civilian contractor and not a government employee, staying in the relatively safe haven of the Green Zone was not an option. Finding that out was a real bummer. My fellow contractors and I were relegated to the Red Zone in Baghdad, the area surrounding the protective Green Zone and beyond. The Red Zone was a normal Arabic city with a mix of upscale homes, shabby houses and dingy shops, and of course a population infiltrated with suspected terrorists. There was little if any assistance given to non-military personnel living in the Red Zone. Any armed protection or fortification of our living quarters was up to us and our company.

Our home was in a company compound, a neighborhood of homes encircled with twelve foot tall concrete walls with barbed wire on top, security cameras and a metal barricade gate that lifted up to let you in, like you would see in a movie at border crossings. There were guys with guns on the ground, on the roofs and at each front door of every home which we had to be buzzed in to. I was starting to get overwhelmed.

MY NEW BEST FRIENDS

The compound where I stayed in Baghdad was a multi-cultural melting pot the likes of which I had never seen or experienced before. The residents were an interesting mix of Americans, Lebanese, Iraqis, Filipinos, Fijians and one New Zealander. The Americans were the owners, company officers and people in charge. The Iraqis and New Zealander worked in the offices doing administrative stuff, maintenance and security. Iraqi women cleaned the rooms. The Lebanese did security, including monitoring the security cameras and communications. The Filipino's did the laundry and the cooking.

My new best friends were the Lebanese, who would be my own personal body guards while I was in Iraq. I later learned the company had arranged for Lebanese men to be my bodyguards when I got to Afghanistan also. I guess they are specialists when it comes to security.

Because of the little French language I had taken in grade school, I could tell my Lebanese PSD friends spoke French when talking on their radios. When I asked them why they did that, they said it was because the Iraqis understand Arabic and probably some English, but not French. They would laugh and say it was their secret code.

I was impressed by the amount of security protection my company was providing for me. It's really hard to put in words what I felt with these guys around who were willing to put themselves between me and a bullet to save my life.

Personal Security Detail (PSD) – Iraq

IRAQI JOB SITE VISITS

After getting settled in the house in Iraq, I found out I needed to go to the Green Zone – before arriving in Afghanistan, I needed to get finger-printed to obtain my DoD (Department of Defense) ID card for clearance to be able to get into Military Bases and to have access to government computers. The signs at the entrance to the Green Zone reading "Do Not Enter or You Will Be Shot" gave me simultaneous feelings of safety and danger. I thought to myself, you're not in Kansas anymore, Toto. Many of the military personnel I met there told me they were advised never to go outside the Green Zone. Looking around and seeing U.S. soldiers toting rifles everywhere was a re- minder of where I was.

Once my body-guards and I were safely inside the secure confines of the Green Zone, We went looking for the finger-printing office. Not expecting a ludicrous problem so soon after my arrival, I was shocked when I was told they had no finger printing ink and they didn't know when they would get more. How could this be? A finger printing office with no ink?

With a little sarcastic humor, I told the MP (Military Police) at the counter I would break open my pen to get the ink out. He failed to see the humor. I explained, I really didn't like putting my life in danger by having to make another trip through the city, but he was obviously perturbed with me. I could tell civilians were merely an inconvenient pain in the ass to him.

The guy's supervisor intervened and politely told us we'd have to go to another base in the Baghdad area to get finger printed. By now, it was getting dark and my bodyguards and I didn't need the extra risk of traveling at night through a war zone, so we decided to hold off until morning.

The next day we traveled to the other base as I really needed to get finger-printed before leaving Iraq and entering Afghanistan. When I and my body-guards walked up to the window and told them what I needed, we were told they were not doing finger-printing that day as the military personnel pointed to the sign below his counter "No Finger Printing on Wednesdays". I would have to come back tomorrow. I couldn't believe this was happening. Frustrated, but trying to be friendly to win his cooperation, I asked the soldier where he was from. He said Washington State. I said, "I'm from Oregon!" I was hoping this would create a comradery so he would help me get what I needed.

I asked to see his commanding officer. When the officer came to the window, I explained why we were at this base and told him we lived in the Red Zone. He understood the danger of us traveling in Baghdad. He told his subordinate to get me finger-printed immediately.

The company I was working for at this juncture was converting many of the existing mansions inside the Green Zone into office buildings, so I did get the chance to spend a little more time inside the Green Zone when I visited those construction sites to see the work first-hand and get to know what quality to expect from local workers when I got to Afghanistan. I also had the opportunity to visit several other job sites outside of Baghdad to see the type of buildings we would be constructing in Afghanistan. I had never seen a container building, also called a "conex," which were often put on trucks and shipped out to the building sites. Some were made out of actual shipping containers like you see on the back of Semi-Trucks here in the USA, and others are manufactured for specific uses such as living quarters, sleeping areas, dining rooms, offices and bath rooms. I learned the local Iraqi workers were escorted into the Green Zone daily and escorted out at the end of the day. This helped prepare me to understand the process of working with local Afghan labor as opposed to working with American labor.

Another phrase I would have to incorporate in my thinking was the use of the term 'mission' with respect to virtually all outings where I would travel from point A to point B for whatever purpose. So, it was not simply going to

be a visit to a job site, it was going to be a mission, just like soldiers going on a mission. Even though I would be going out there to build structures, it was still a mission with many of the same military safety implications and threats such as road-side bombs and attacks by terrorists.

As we drove on missions to see jobs outside the city, we saw nothing but desert with intermittent green patches, the occasional oasis showing there was water. Dust and sand covered 99% of what we saw. Occasionally, alongside the road by dried up ponds, I saw locals raking stuff into white piles and wondered what it was. I learned they were raking salt, harvesting to sell.

The locals used donkeys to pull all kinds of carts and there were sheep and goats all along the roads. Roadside shops were built out of any available material and sold everything from tires and gas to food. It reminded me of what a third world country must look like. Then I realized – wake up! I am in a third-world country!

GERMANY – A SIDE TRIP

There were all these American military bases in Iraq and yet for some reason none of them could process and issue my DoD Badge (CAC card). I found out I had to travel to Ramstad Air Force Base in Germany, by myself, to get it. The closest I had ever come to Germany was out of college when I visited Sweden where my grandfather was from. I had no clue where I was going.

Back on a plane, my first layover was in Jordan to meet with the vice president of our company in charge of finances at the company office in Amman. I was met by a Jordanian employee who walked me through the process of getting my Visa and delivered me to the company office. As we traveled through the countryside, I asked him about his family and his country. He told me he did not make enough money yet to get married and was working as hard as he could to change that.

There seemed to be more green patches and grazing land than in Iraq plus big beautiful mansions. I noticed all the street signs and billboards were in both Arabic and English. This shocked me. Once in Amman, I learned many Americans working in Iraq brought their families, wives and children to live there while they commuted back and forth. The city was very modern, similar to a city in southern California, and supposed to be very safe.

The office was a condo where I was to stay and work till my late night flight to Germany. The company president asked me to transfer my hand written notes onto "the Word program" on the computer. I explained I did not know that program, I only knew AutoCAD (an architectural drawing program on the computer) so to compensate that, he said he would send me an assistant when I got to Afghanistan. The president laughed as he modified my documents saying something like, "Who is working for whom here?"

Late in the night I was back to the airport and off to Germany. Of all the Arabic cities I had seen so far, I liked Amman the best, even better than Dubai.

Arriving in Germany was just like arriving at any other airport in America except most of the signs were in German, some in English. I found the shuttle to the rental cars, as I had to drive myself to the Air Force base and back. I was so glad they spoke English. It was a two-hour drive to get to the base, so the attendant assigned me a car with a GPS. Not only did I not know where I was going, but when the attendant ran my bank card, he told me there was not enough money in the account. Now I'm panicking. How much was this car costing me? He told me they need a $1,500 deposit that would be refunded when I brought the car back. For one day? What to do? I hoped I could reach my wife. I also hoped the company would reimburse me as I had not received a pay check yet, I've purchased clothes, sleeping bag, medical shots. I was starting to worry. Luckily, my cell phone had the global chip. Shirley transferred the funds instantly online. Man, I dodged that bullet. Now I understood why I saw a young US military wife with a couple children crying at the car rental place... because she didn't have the money for the deposit for a rental car and was trying to figure out what to do, how to get to her husband's military base. I got the car, the attendant set up the GPS for me and I was on my way.

Driving through this part of Germany looked just like home in Portland, Oregon except I was going 80 to 90 miles per hour on the Autobahn freeway and cars were passing me like I was standing still.

I reached the town near the US Air Base where I had to stop and wait for a phone call from my Baghdad office telling me that my paperwork had gone through in the USA and I could proceed onto the base. Pulling into a Burger King and yes, they took US currency, I then drove to the waiting area outside the base gate where I met a retired US Air Force Colonel whose wife taught school on the Air Base. They had family in Oregon and Washington. What are the odds of that?

We talked a couple hours, then he had to leave and I got the phone call to get escorted on base. I got turned away at the gate because I didn't have my DoD badge. I explained I was there to get my DoD badge. They sent me to the visitor center to get a pass. Then I called the escort again but she was gone. Her office said they would not take the responsibility for me and the visitor center said unless someone came to the visitor center to escort me onto the base, they would not give me a pass. I was stuck. Finally, I reached the right person on base who told the visitor center to let me on base because I was an American and I had a US Passport. I had to rush – the DoD office was to close in 10 minutes.

I quickly found out the base was huge. I found the right building but there was no place to park, all restricted and permit only. I finally found a place to park and ran the quarter mile to the building, getting to the door at 4:00, closing time. The doors were still open. Rushing to the desk, I could barely talk as I was so out of breath from running. The person at the desk said I was too late, they were closed. I pleaded with her, explaining I just needed the card to get on the bases in Afghanistan and that I had come all the way from Baghdad through the night and was leaving that evening for Dubai and then Afghanistan. She said she would make an exception and process my paperwork. I got my card! I was beginning to realize nothing is easy in this business and to always be ready for something to go wrong. Adapt and persevere was to be my new motto.

I left the Air Force base with a sigh of relief. I had my card. Mission accomplished.

Now back to the airport, after filling the car with gas. None of the gas pumps looked like ours and I didn't know what kind of gas to put in the car. No one spoke English. I tried a few words of German and Swedish, asking people, "sprichst du Englisch?" following with "anyone speak English?" Finally, a person told me to open the gas cap and it should tell me which gas to use. I opened it and yup, it had 95 and something in German on it. I looked at the gas pumps and found a 93. Close enough for me. I filled up the tank. Finally, with my DoD Badge, I made it to the German airport and waited for my flight to Dubai.

ON TO THE FINAL DESTINATION - AFGHANISTAN

The two weeks I had spent in Iraq and my quick trip to Germany were anything but restful, but in retrospect they gave me an excellent preparation course for what awaited me in Afghanistan. At least I was able to call my wife by cell-phone or Skype every day.

Once in Dubai and at the hotel, I met up with my security guy, who went with me to get my Afghanistan visa from the Afghan embassy in Dubai. We first found a creepy little hole in the wall photo place with a booth to get my pictures for my visa and several more I would need for documents at the Kabul airport to get into the country. The picture booth was the same you find at amusement parks in America.

Next, we were off to the Afghan Embassy. It was down a crummy part of town, a small one story building with what looked like Taliban all over in the waiting room. The man behind the glassed counter told my security they wanted my passport and to come back later. I asked my security, "Are you sure?" I was afraid I would not get it back. We hung around outside for a while and went back in. I had no idea what was being said, as my security guy was speaking in Arabic. He told me they worked it out and he paid them money and I got my passport back with an Afghan visa. I was now ready to go to Afghanistan the next day.

When I was finally on the plane headed to Kabul, I felt like it had taken months of traveling all over the world to get to that point, and I still didn't really know what my job was. All I knew for sure was that I would manage construction contracts for the company and build "stuff." As I had been told before, I would have to figure it out when I got there.

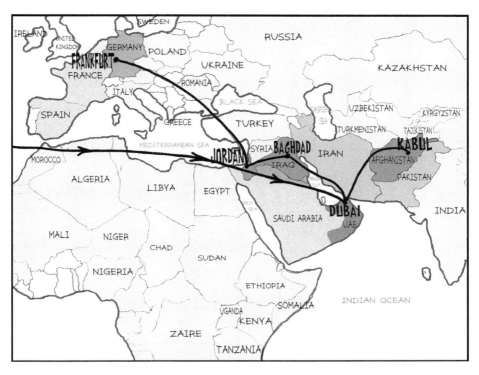

Travel from USA to Dubai - to Iraq - to Jordan - to Germany - back to Dubai - finally to Afghanistan

CHAPTER 3

Welcome to Afghanistan, Mr. Rich

"All experiences, especially into new territory are scary."
—Sally Ride, U.S. Astronaut

As I arrived in Kabul, Afghanistan on Safi Airlines, I looked down and saw the mountains and desert I had so often seen on television and couldn't believe I was actually there. The terrain looked like a combination of Tucson, Arizona and eastern Colorado, mostly bare ground and rocks.

Just as in Baghdad, the planes were parked away from the brand new terminal to avoid any "two-for-the price-of-one" devastation that could result from Taliban rocket attacks. We had to walk this time from the plane to the terminal concourse.

My company sent a bodyguard with me from Dubai to Afghanistan. Once inside the terminal at Kabul, we met an Afghan General who walked us through customs. He had soft dark eyes with a twinkle in them and a square body that matched his gentle square face with short cropped hair and a heavy black mustache. He wore a black business suit jacket over a long oversized black & gold print shirt with the top buttons unbuttoned, resembling a baggy martial arts shirt. Underneath that, his baggy black pants hid the socks he wore inside his sandals on his feet.

I then met my new set of Lebanese bodyguards. They had close cropped hair and beards or goatees circling their mouths wearing sunglasses and wore tan bullet-proof vests pulled over black t-shirts tucked into khaki pants with more pockets than normal pulled over hiking boots. They each toted several weapons, including AK-47's. When we got into the car they had me put on a bullet proof vest. This time, I knew how. For some unknown reason, I already liked Afghanistan better than Iraq. I don't know why, but Afghanistan somehow had a friendlier feel to it.

Since I did not know any Middle Eastern languages, the company assigned me an Afghan interpreter. He would go with us everywhere and interpret for me and my Lebanese PSD, who spoke Arabic but not the native Afghan languages, Dari and Pashto. I ended up picking up a little Dari (a type of Farsi-Iranian language) in my travels, but in the beginning, I didn't know a word. Pashto is used by the Pashtuns who live mostly across southern and eastern Afghanistan. It was obvious that the language barrier was another of the major challenges I would have while conducting business in my new environment.

Our little convoy drove through the congested streets of Kabul to our compound.

KABUL

Kabul sprawls out over a hill and down into a valley. It overlooks a tall mountain range in the distance. I would not call the city of Kabul modern by any standard in comparison to North America. There are parts of the city where living conditions are passable by modern day standards and others that are basically slums. Rickety open-air shops and dilapidated business structures are everywhere you look lining the roads. The streets themselves are very busy – not just with cars, but with bicyclists weighed down with items like auto tires to be fixed, and crowds of pedestrians. Driving down the streets, blocks of broken concrete are scattered alongside the sidewalks and buildings where once colorful paint has long since faded in the heat of the sun. Buildings had advertisements plastered on the walls where people passing by could see them – but the advertisements do nothing to hide the variety of colors the tin roofs are built of or that the buildings the advertisements rest on are now covered in a layer of dirt. Some buildings that once sported advertisements high above the doorways of shops have nothing left but the torn corners of the posters from where they were once stapled. Below them, under the cover of colorful awnings, shops hide in the shade, lining the sidewalks.

Streets of Kabul (Copyright © Alan Buffard used with permission)

The main city streets are paved and the rest of the streets are dirt, which makes things very dusty except when they are snow-covered. The air quality in Kabul is a serious health hazard. Winters are exceptionally bad because a lot of Afghans use any means whatsoever to generate heat, such as burning plastic bottles. This leads to people having "Kabul cough," a common condition in the city.

Traffic is dense most of the time with cars and trucks driving on both sides of the streets, weaving in and out and barely missing head-on collisions – with occasional unfortunate exceptions. It's just one of many ways to die in Kabul, aside from the Taliban, of course.

Despite the run-down feeling of the main roads and sidewalks, Kabul is also home to beautiful mosques that people flock to, with bright colors giving the sense that the buildings were much different than the shops and houses lining the streets. It is not only the largest city in Afghanistan – Kabul is terribly overcrowded with a population of over 3.5 million – but it's also the nation's capital. Kabul is over 3,500 years old.

Most of the shopping is done in open markets like a Farmers market mixed with little shops, particularly in an area called "Chicken Street," where all kinds of merchandise are on display for sale night and day. There are many streets, with each street specializing in a particular category of goods such as kitchen utensils, meat, vegetables, spices – each had its own street. There were plumbing supplies on one street, lumber in another, furniture in a side alleyway, and almost anything else you could need for the Afghan way of life.

There were hordes of flies everywhere. I found it to be a terrible issue, especially in the oppressive heat of the summer months. Picture for a moment an outdoor market with raw, unrefrigerated meat hanging everywhere and covered with flies.

While not as prevalent as flies, sand storms are another major irritant. I always tried to be inside somewhere when sand storms were about to hit. It is like being sand-blasted and the sand gets into everything because it is so fine. We frequently had to keep our computers covered because the sand could easily ruin them.

Many of the buildings and houses are fortified in some manner or at the very least have armed guards outside. There is one section of Kabul where modern condo buildings had been springing up for the wealthier Afghan business people and famous local celebrities to buy. One of the Afghan companies I worked with was building some of these, so I was able to get a tour. Structurally, they looked solid and the interior finishes appeared to be similar in quality to American condos.

New Condos in Kabul

Some housing was built right into the hillside surrounding Kabul similar to the Pueblo Indian cliff cities in the Southwestern United States. The only way up to those homes was by a trail or path; there were no streets or roads.

Kabul Hillside Housing (Copyright © Jim Ellis used with permission)

Moving away from the central city of Kabul to the outskirts, dirt streets become even more common, with paved roads few and far between. Housing changes to more rudimentary mud construction in what we Americans would consider the countryside, and there are nomads who still travel with their livestock and live in tents like they did 2,000 years ago. Camels, sheep and goats are quite commonplace outside the city.

There were small children everywhere in Afghanistan, wandering around searching for food and almost anything they could find. But one hazard they face are the land mines placed here and there by the Russians, Taliban and other terrorists.

Little Girl (Copyright © Jim Ellis used with permission)

THE RUSSIAN AFTERMATH

During the 1980s, long before the Taliban insurgency, the Russians had fought a long and bloody war with Afghanistan in an attempt to conquer the country. In the movie *Charlie Wilson's War*, the U.S. aided Afghanistan in defeating the Russians, ending their influence over the Afghans.

In my travels around the country, I witnessed many parts of the landscape littered with remnants of that ten-year struggle. I saw scores of Russian military junk yards with planes, jets, tanks and equipment the Russians left behind when they pulled out. There are thousands of yet-to-explode Russian land mines still in the ground all over the country. It was not unusual to have land mine explosions around the city of Kabul and the surrounding countryside. Land mines remain even around some of the U.S. military bases, many of which are former Russian bases. Many of these bases were sites for reconstruction projects I was supervising. When starting construction projects, we had to sweep for mines and get them removed before bringing in equipment, materials and workers.

Russian Junkyards

One of the abandoned Russian military bases taken over by the U.S. is Bagram Airfield (BAF). Personnel from all over the world are now stationed at Bagram. I visited this base many times during my four years in Afghanistan for meetings on projects both on and off the base. Each time we came to BAF, we had to be cleared by the security officer. While they were clearing me to enter, I had to wait outside the protective walls, in plain sight in a wide open gravel field. I thought it was a bunch of crap, to put it politely. They could have at least let me wait in a secure area inside the wire while being cleared. We could have been shot or rocketed at any time.

WELCOME TO AFGHANISTAN

It quickly became crystal clear that this job in Afghanistan would test me more than anything had in my life.

On my first day in Kabul, a suspected Afghan warlord, with short cropped mixture of white/light gray hair and beard, standing a few inches shy of six feet tall, showed up at our front door with a bunch of his tribesmen. His presence was a stark contrast from the scenery of his tribesmen outside with his traditional business Afghan attire – crispy white long loose top over white, baggy pajama-like pants and a long loose black sleeveless vest. The tribesmen who accompanied him appeared younger with very dark hair and wore dark clothes, complete with heavy jackets and dark headdresses. Each carried weapons with them, some carrying more than one.

He demanded money my company supposedly owed him for a construction project he had done for them. The angry and heavily armed man implied that if I did not give him the $35,000 he was owed, he would cut off the heads of everyone in the house and burn the house down. I was petrified!

Quickly calling the company's main office and explaining my plight, I was relieved to learn they would get me the money right away. It seemed the man who had the country manager position before me had bolted with the cash instead of paying the warlord. The next few days were very tense until my security sat at the coffee table counting out the cash payment with the warlord's henchmen and my bodyguards looking on with weapons in hand. It was a far cry from transacting a deal back home in America. I not only had to be concerned about Taliban on the roads, but also warlords coming to the house.

As he left, I looked outside and saw the street lined with his tribesmen, all armed. My Lebanese bodyguards laughed, "Welcome to Afghanistan, Mr. Rich!" I would be reminded of this phrase over and over again during my entire time in Afghanistan.

I was told by an Afghan businessman that there are four things you need to understand about doing business in Afghanistan:

1. People will lie to you

2. People will cheat you

3. People will steal from you

4. People will want to kill you

He told me that if I based my actions on these four principles, I'd do fine.

In the blur of the first few days at Kabul House, someone also gave me this *Afghan Survival Guide*:

AFGHAN SURVIVAL GUIDE

ONLY YOU are responsible for your safety. Your actions will determine your future.

HEALTH – People working under pressure must keep themselves in excellent physical condition. You must allow time for relaxation, even if this means putting off important work. Get regular periods of leave because the physical affects the mental.

CONDUCT – Avoid behavior likely to arouse suspicion. Cameras, binoculars and tape recorders should be used with discretion and only after necessary permission has been granted.

OFFICIAL PROPERTY – When faced with an attacker whose main purpose seems to be looting rather than physical harm, DO NOT PUT THE LIVES of the staff in jeopardy over protecting organization equipment.

KEEP YOUR HEAD DOWN – If there is danger avoid the instinct to see what is going on, do not expose yourself and do not move unless you're going from a place of greater danger to a place of less danger.

MINE AWARENESS – Afghanistan is the most heavily mined country in the world. There are battlefields everywhere with unexploded ordinances (UXO) and or land mines. 150 to 300 people are injured or killed by mines or UXO every month in Afghanistan.

Now I knew I was living in the danger zone.

The home in Afghanistan was a modest residential dwelling in Kabul, called the Kabul House. It was surrounded on three sides with an eight foot high concrete block wall with razor wire wound up on top. Our yard was small but was kept in good condition. It reminded me of San Diego, a stucco home, warm with lots of greenery, complete with a grape arbor and almond tree, unlike the rest of the Kabul area which seemed dusty and dirty. There was a huge generator in the front yard that powered the house and my office when we lost city electrical power several times a day. I would have to learn to operate the generator whenever it was needed.

Kabul House

Metal bars enclosed the stairway to the bedrooms and there was a metal gate at the top of the stairs. If we were attacked, we were to lock the gate at the top of the stairs and fall back to my room, as my two Lebanese body-guards would defend us the best they could with their AK-47s.

The living room, dining room, kitchen & a bathroom were on the main floor. Our home had a full finished basement with one more bedroom and another bath plus another room we housed our weapons in that we called the Armory. In the side yard was a storage building that had been converted to my office.

It was obvious that many things in that country had not changed in hundreds of years. During the first week, there were carpenters working on building shelves and remodeling our house. It became evident to me that something that would take a day to build in America would take several days in Afghanistan as they were using the same tools my great-great grandfather used in Sweden 200 years ago. I have a couple of those old tools at home.

My job for the company was to go online to the USACE (U.S. Army Corps of Engineers) and other U.S. government websites each day and find upcoming projects to bid on. I had to go through each proposal request, looking for anything that might spell trouble, and prepare the requests for local Afghan sub-contractors to bid on. These had to include armed security guards for protecting the workers at the sites. Again, not your typical item on a cost sheet.

Many buildings and housing units both on and off military bases and at construction sites, were being built out of conex containers, similar to those I had seen on construction sites around Baghdad. The containers came in two basic sizes (8'x20' and 8'x40') and had holes cut in them for windows and doors. Partition walls inside created individual rooms. Electrical wiring, heating/air conditioning units and bathroom and kitchen fixtures were then added to turn them into complete living quarters.

Multiple conex units can be stacked on each other with external stairways added to provide access to the upper floors. Because of their diverse usage and transportability, there were manufacturing plants set up in Afghanistan to make custom conex buildings. I myself would go on to design and oversee construction projects using conex containers for temporary housing and offices on construction projects and on military bases. They were delivered by truck to the site, quick to assemble, and easy to secure with guards to protect the construction workers from Taliban attacks.

SECURITY AT KABUL HOUSE

Kabul House was quite a distance from any military base. I was not allowed to answer the bell at the front gate. Whenever that gate was opened I had to run out of sight. And I wasn't allowed to walk down the street without a bodyguard.

I was told I needed to grow a beard to fit in more with the locals so I would blend in and not draw attention to myself. Clean shaven Americans made for fun target practice. We traveled in a very low profile manner whenever we ventured out – no heavily armored vehicles and no visible weapons.

Mr. Rich American Style/ Mr, Rich Afghan Style

Besides my personal Lebanese PSD's, who lived in the house with me, my company hired a local Afghan security firm to protect our house during the day and go out with us on missions, but the Afghan security all returned to their homes at night. There were generally three to five Afghan bodyguards around the perimeter, with two or three of those accompanying me when I traveled for meetings or out to job sites. The Afghan security guys were generally from the northern tribes, who were on our side against the Taliban when we first entered the country, and were not afraid to fight and die. This was all part of the cost of doing business in a war zone.

Many times I had business meetings at the house, and I found it interesting that the Afghan businessmen would always ask me if I had enough guns. They assured me that whenever I needed more guns they would be happy to give them to me. Can you imagine this being a topic of conversation during a business meeting in America?

Afghan Bodyguards - Ready to go to a Business Meeting

Just like when I went out on missions to visit sites in Iraq, we traveled in Afghanistan by convoy, just not with as many cars and bodyguards. We took two cars. One carried me and my trusted Lebanese bodyguards and a second car driven by our Afghan interpreter carried a few Afghan security guards. As we were always zooming down the road hell bent for leather at up to a hundred miles an hour, I just had to ask the same question I had asked my drivers in Iraq.

"Why are you guys always driving so fast?"

The answer I got was only a slightly different version of the response I got in Iraq: "Well, this way it is harder for the terrorists to time the explosion of a bomb when they attempt to blow up our car. Hopefully, if it does go off, it will be behind us and not under us or in front of us."

My Lebanese friends would then chuckle, "Welcome to Afghanistan Mr. Rich."

Most of the Afghan security guards didn't speak English, so my interpreter would have to give them directions.

I always wondered whether the Muslim Afghan security guards (who went home every night) would stay and fight or decide to run away if we were attacked. Why would they risk their lives for me, an American? There was no doubt in my mind that my Christian Lebanese bodyguards (who lived with me in our home) would fight to the death to protect me.

There were times when the word on the street was that we might be attacked by the Taliban soon. For such occasions, I had what I called my 'running pack' which was my small backpack holding my laptop computer and a few essentials. If needed, I could grab my backpack and run. Sometimes I slept in my clothes in case we had to make a run for it in the middle of the night. As you can imagine, I would not sleep well after being told, "Mr. Rich, have your running pack ready tonight."

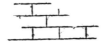

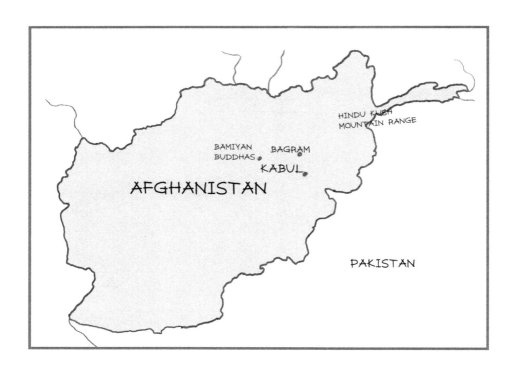

CHAPTER 4

Kabul House - The Cast of Characters

"The best way to cheer yourself is to try to cheer somebody else up."
—Mark Twain

Living at Kabul House was an experience like none I had ever been through. The group of men I lived with varied widely in nationality, culture, race and religion - all very memorable and genuine in their own way. It was like being in a multi-cultural combination soap opera and sit-com.

BABA, THE GATEKEEPER

One of the first persons I met upon my arrival was our gatekeeper, who actually came with the house. Standing just under six feet tall, Baba was built very lean, always wearing a little brown wool hat rolled up enough with his cropped white hair peeking out showing his saddened crinkled dark eyes under thick bushy eyebrows and a medium length thick coarse white-gray beard. I thought he was much older than I, until one day I learned he was actually more than 10 years younger. The owner had been paying him a mere pittance to watch the house, but when my company rented it, they paid him a decent wage to stay on to guard our gate. We called him "Baba" which means "Grandfather." He was so proud of the full dark green uniform our security chief gave him that he wore it every day. Baba gave me a Pakol hat like his as a gift, a traditional Afghan thick soft round-topped wool hat rolled up to fit snug similar like a beret, worn by the local tribesmen in the North.

Baba with Pakol Hat

Baba would pat down all guests, our cook, and anyone else wanting to enter our gate. He took his job seriously, searching them for weapons before they could enter the front yard. He also patted down all workers as they were leaving to make sure they were not stealing anything. He and I became great friends quickly, greeting each other in Dari every morning. He did not live in the house with the rest of us but would come to work every morning except Friday. Friday is a holy day in Afghanistan, and the only day of the week the Afghans do not work.

Baba once told me that if the Taliban attacked our house, he would cut my head off quickly and put it in a clean hole (our water well). I thought this was a strange token until he explained a Talib would torture me, cutting my head off very slowly and stuffing it in the crap hole (the sewer).

I thanked Baba for the well-intentioned gesture but asked my interpreter to make it clear to him that he was not to jump the gun on cutting my head off but to wait until the very last minute. After all, what looks like an attack might end up being Taliban simply running by our house without stopping to lop off any heads. Fortunately, Baba could relate and agreed to wait till the last minute before sending me off to heaven.

One horrific day, Baba's nine-year-old son was run over by a military convoy, supposedly a U.S. convoy. We all freaked because we didn't know what Baba would do. We had my interpreter take Baba and his son to the hospital, where his son soon died. My interpreter then took Baba and his son home to where they would prepare him and bury him. We later found out it was not a U.S. military convoy, but another country's convoy. The tragedy of Baba's son's death was awful and yet he showed up for work the very next day. He didn't want to get fired as he needed to support his family and this was the best job he'd ever had. We had to convince him to go home and stay home for however long the grieving period was and we would still pay him.

MY LEBANESE BODY GUARDS – RONY AND RABIH

The two Lebanese personal body guards assigned to protect me, 24-7, were Rony and Rabih, who lived in the house full time. They told me they had been fighting in one war or another since they were about 10 years old. Rony was riddled with bullet scars from head to toe. He even had a rocket hit him one time and stick into him, but it didn't go off. He was unable to walk for a long period of time because of this. They loved to show off their scars and their tattoos.

Rony and Rabih were Christians like me. Both were tall, Rabih built very lean and Rony a bit bulkier. Both men were energetic, wore t-shirts and khaki pants, had short, black hair with thin trimmed beards, dark expressive eyebrows and sparkling eyes that danced. They had been fierce and brutal warriors in battle and yet compassionate to the less fortunate, especially considerate of underprivileged children, "No one deserves this type of life," one of them said, "but that is the way it has been for 1,000 years and it ain't changin' any time soon."

There were what I called "Street Kids" that came and picked up our garbage every Friday. They would also go through the open sewers looking for stuff. Some are orphans and some are the sole means of support for their family. We paid them to take the garbage away. On Fridays my PSD's would invite them in and feed them. On one occasion one of the little boys spilled his soda and ran to leave as he thought we would get mad at him. We brought him back with him crying and explained "No Problem" and poured him another soda.

Street Kids Having Lunch in our Kabul compound

In their late 30's, Rony has a wife and two children at home in Lebanon. Rabih, married with no children, also has a home in Lebanon.

They smoked a lot as I had to keep reminding them to not smoke in the house. I am a non-smoker and couldn't stand the smell inside. Both would laugh when I brought this up, saying I should be more concerned about getting lead poisoning (jokingly referring to bullets hitting me) than being harmed by cigarette smoke.

They were always putting themselves in between me and any strangers nearby. One time I was standing on the roof of a building discussing construction with the Afghan contractor and Rony kept pushing me around. I got pretty irritated and told him to knock it off. "But I am just trying to protect you Mr. Rich. It makes it harder for the snipers to hit you if you keep moving." I never complained about it again.

One night when our neighborhood was under a rocket attack, I heard a rocket go right by my bedroom window behind my head and hit the house next door. The Lebanese came running into my room to see if I was OK. I was sitting on the edge of my bed saying something they could not understand. I am sure I was saying something like "What the hell is going on?" but my English was too fast for them to understand. They thought I was praying to Jesus. At times when other Lebanese guards would come over to visit, they would tell them about the "not so brave Mr. Rich praying to Jesus for his life during a rocket attack" and they would all have a big laugh. I just let them have their fun.

One of the Lebanese guards brought a Turkish coffee pot from his home, with a set of cups and made Turkish coffee every morning and night. We would sit in the yard relaxing and talk, drinking our Turkish coffee. "Excuse me, could you pass the coffee? Hey, was that a mortar that just went off?" I was surprised how nonchalant I became after only a month or so in Kabul. "No Mr. Rich that was a 180 rocket," one of them might say to correct me.

Turkish Coffee with Rony & Rabih

Over coffee, we would talk for hours about our families back home and how each of us grew up. History with our different perspectives and discussing our common devotion to Christian beliefs was like a breath of fresh air given our Islamic surroundings.

It is really hard to explain the workings of your mind when you know how you could easily be killed at any moment. People talk about being a heartbeat away from eternity, but living in this high risk environment brings that feeling to the forefront with tremendous clarity. It truly was our faith in God that carried us through those perilous days.

They liked to play around out in the yard at night. After talking about satellites, how they zoom in to Earth, they'd look up at the stars, cup their mouths and yell, "Hey you guys in America, Mr. Rich is our good friend. Please send in the F-16's if we are attacked!" It was refreshing to laugh and joke.

They told me they would protect me with their lives, and I asked them what would happen if it came to a battle where the Taliban outnumbered us heavily and captured us. They said that first they would be killed and then the Taliban would cut my head off very slowly. I asked them if it came to that and if they were still barely alive, would they shoot me so I would die quickly and escape that slow torture?

With some apprehension in their voices, they told me no, they would not do that.

"We have sworn to protect you Mr. Rich, and that would be murder and we would go to hell. You don't want us to go to hell, do you? And besides, Mr. Rich, quit being such a baby. It will all be over in 15 minutes and we will be waiting for you in heaven, and then we will all be eating lamb together in Paradise." Was that supposed to comfort me?

My security detail are the ones that helped me disguise my American appearance and blend in with the Afghan society. Besides urging me to grow a beard and wear an Afghan scarf, they even had an Afghan-type vest made for me by a tailor in Kabul. I wore some of the local clothes and scarves to blend in as much as possible.

During my time at Kabul House, one or both of the Lebanese body-guards were with me during every waking hour and always had weapons ready. They never complained about the need to protect me constantly. Well, almost never. I was having an early breakfast with Rony one Friday morning and he said, "Mr. Rich, do you really have to get up so early on Fridays when no one is working? When we hear your feet hit the floor in the morning, we have to get up right away. Do you think we could all sleep in on Fridays?"

I guess I never really thought about my feet hitting the floor being their mandatory wake-up call, so I decided to stay in my room on Friday mornings and read so they could sleep.

They say in the Middle East your name reflects who and what you are. So my name, Mr. Rich, meant to many of them that I was wealthy. I would hear that time and time again whenever I was introduced as Mr. Rich. People would look at me in awe and ask me just how wealthy I was. I would have to explain I was not wealthy, but it was difficult squishing their first impression and getting them to believe me.

One day I explained to Rony and Rabih that my real name was not Rich but Richard. There was dead silence and they had worried looks on their faces.

They asked, "Your name is really Richard?"

Their obvious concern caused me to take a step back and reach into the depths of the memories from my college history studies. In a flash it came to me. They were associating the name Richard with King Richard the Lion Hearted from the crusades. History told us King Richard had killed thousands of Muslims during those holy wars.

With a look of deep concern on their faces, they told me not to tell anyone in Afghanistan my name is Richard.

"The Taliban will burn down our house and want to kill you more than if you were Jewish," they warned.

I had a tough time comprehending that this Muslim hatred for Richard the Lion Hearted could still be that strong over something that happened over a thousand years ago.

They further told me the Lebanese had so much respect for Richard the Lion Hearted they would not name a son Richard. Different cultures, different rules.

SAFI, THE COOK

Our cook did not live in the house with us but walked to work every day. He was about a head shorter than me. Safi had a clean look with a soft face, brown eyes, short black hair, a mustache and very short shaved beard around his jawline. In the kitchen he wore a white shirt with sleeves rolled up to his elbows and a tan apron hanging loosely around his neck tied around his back over baggy black pajama-like pants and sandals. Safi was originally from Afghanistan and moved his family to Pakistan for several years while Afghanistan was ruled by the Taliban. He returned when the Taliban lost control. He spoke very little English, leaving me to use my interpreter to communicate with him.

One day as I came into the kitchen, I noticed Safi scrubbing the floor with an odd colored rag and didn't think anything of it. But a few days later, I came into the kitchen as he was preparing the rice for dinner and noticed the same rag again. But this time, it was sitting under the lid of the rice pot to keep the lid steady while the water was boiling.

Trying to be as diplomatic as I could, I told Safi that using that same rag he washed the floor with on the rice was making me sick.

"No problem Mr. Rich, I take care of it." I was very familiar with that phrase because he used it whenever I asked him to make any changes in the kitchen.

The next day at lunch I was eating the rice and it tasted funny again but this time it had kind of a bleach odor to it. I went into the kitchen and saw the same rag on the rice pot. I pointed at it and shrugged my shoulders as if to say, "What's up with that?" With his usual big smile, Safi quickly said again, "No problem Mr. Rich." Reaching under the kitchen sink, he pulled out a bottle of bleach, poured some on the rag, wrung it out by hand and placed the rag back on the rice. He grinned at me like he was expecting a round of applause. Trying not to crush his spirit, I politely took the rag and threw it into the garbage.

"No more rags on the rice, OK?" He just nodded quietly in agreement.

EATING AFGHAN STYLE

Although bland, the standard Afghan food was quite colorful with all the vegetables, such as cucumbers, tomatoes, corn, okra, green beans, brown beans, and potatoes, as well as various sauces. The meat was usually chicken or Lamb and sometimes goat.

We had to keep reminding Safi to use bottled water for cooking because the local tap water would make us non-Afghans sick. I had diarrhea 2-3 times a week and was taking huge doses of Imodium. I jokingly called it the Afghan diet because I lost 30 pounds right away. And it wasn't only the water that made us sick. There was rice at every meal, which often had raisins mixed in. The local rice was not your garden variety Uncle Ben's type; it was spiced up with bugs and other impurities. The cook would place the meals on the table at about the same time every day wrapping the food on the table with saran wrap to keep the flies off. We had fly traps and those sticky fly strips hanging everywhere. My Lebanese guards laughingly warned me that if a raisin moved it was really a fly and if it did not, it was OK to eat. We quickly obtained our own jasmine rice that came from outside the country for the cook to use, so we no longer had to differentiate flies from raisins.

I finally got so tired of the same old stuff every day that I asked Safi to change things up a little and make something different. He said he'd be happy to do that. As I waited in anticipation at the next meal, he came out of the kitchen with a bunch of the normal round bowls and then he went back and brought out an oblong bowl just for me. With a big smile, he set the oblong bowl in front of me as if to say, voila! While the bowl was of a different shape, what was in it looked the same as all the others had. With my interpreter's help, I said, "I don't want to be rude, but this looks like the same stuff in a different shaped bowl."

"Oh no, Mr. Rich, yours has a few more pieces of chicken in it," he replied proudly. I just had to laugh it off and realize I would have no impact on the menu. The local cuisine would just have to do.

We had fresh Afghan flatbread at every meal that our interpreter picked up at the bread shop on the corner. Bread shops are everywhere in Kabul. Some of the bakers prepare the bread on the floor using their feet. So, it was not uncommon for me to come into the kitchen and see the cook cutting and preparing the food directly on the floor. I'm sure the Afghans didn't see anything wrong with that because that is the way they do it in their home, as well as eating sitting on the floor.

Corner Bread Store (Copyright © Jim Ellis used with permission)

On Fridays, Safi's day off, Rony and Robih would make traditional Lebanese meals for us once in a while. I liked the Lebanese food and welcomed the change. But when it came to beverages, Rony and Rabih were as Americanized as it gets, consuming Coca-Cola by the gallons.

Since the cook only prepared the lunch and dinner meals, I was on my own for breakfast. Eggs were one of the foods we had to screen very carefully for quality because, while many impurities did not bother the locals, they did make the rest of us very sick.

I'd bypass the eggs for breakfast, I would have flat bread and oatmeal that I sometimes bought at the western store in Kabul. It was expensive, but a reminder of home, and it was worth it to me.

That became my routine meal until I read the fine print on a milk carton, noticing it was from the next door country, Pakistan, and had an expiration date several months into the future. I jokingly called it "nuke milk" after that, figuring it was treated with nuclear waste from Pakistan to make it last so long. So much for the milk on my oatmeal. I finally got some peanut butter at a US base, Camp Phoenix, to spread on my flat bread. The Afghans could not believe I would put peanut butter on their bread. For some reason they could not stand peanut butter. From then on, I would have only that and bottled water on my oatmeal for breakfast.

On some Fridays we liked to have barbeques, opening up opportunities to invite people over for a 'meet and greet'. Our guests included officials from the Afghan government, Generals in the Afghan Army, and fellow western-ers working in Afghanistan for other companies and government organiza-tions. The westerners included Americans, Canadians, Europeans, Austra-lians, New Zealanders, and South Africans. I'd invite anybody I met.

These were more than just barbeques. They were my Kabul version of a networking get-together. We would have barbequed lamb and chicken, and ground up lamb instead of beef hamburgers, but of course, no pork. The Leb-anese would always make fun of how much barbequed food I could eat. They joked with the others about how I could probably eat a whole lamb by myself.

ZERMINA, THE CLEANING LADY

Our cleaning lady, who was also our part time cook, was a widow with four children. I learned that her husband had most likely been killed by the Tali-ban since they took him away and he never came back.

(Copyright © Jim Ellis used with permission)

Zermina made the two-hour walk to our house every day in her blue burka, covering her from head to toe. Only her eyes peeked out. No one in her family, except her mother, knew she worked for us. Women were not allowed to work in a building occupied only by men, and those violating that rule might easily be killed as punishment. We had to keep her out of the sight of the Afghans that came to our house. If any recognized her, she could be in big trouble, even putting her life in danger.

Once inside our gate, Zermina took off the burka she wore over her work clothes which were dark print layered scarf-like loose fitting full-length dresses having both her arms and legs covered. Above that she always wore her hair tucked inside a very long matching print scarf wrapped around her head and neck, draped over her shoulders and down her back. Her square face with a short nose and dark eyes showed sadness, that the years had not been kind to her, yet you could see glimpses of her in her prime. She then started on her chores for the day, which consisted of cleaning house, doing our laundry and helping in the kitchen.

Zermina and I would try to teach each other our languages on a daily basis. We also had to teach her how to do many common everyday tasks, like even washing her hands when working in the kitchen. Good hygiene and housekeeping habits were foreign to her. Similar to the case of our cook, the housekeeping skills of our cleaning lady made for constant "can you believe this" emails I'd write home. Keep in mind that she lives in a mud house so good hygiene and housekeeping habits were foreign to her. My security and I had to teach her the proper way to clean things around the house. One day walking by the bathroom, I heard her singing as she was cleaning. I watched in horror as she scrubbed the toilet with a brush, and then used the same brush to clean the sink and then the mirror, and then the cups that held our tooth brushes. Another reason I would get constant diarrhea. I practically lived on Imodium, Tums and Pepto Bismol. I could hardly keep from laughing out loud and when I told the others how she cleaned their toothbrush cups, they nearly got sick. I suggested to my interpreter to get her to make a few adjustments to her cleaning routine.

Because she did our laundry, one day my interpreter came to me with her crying. She had used bleach on one of my shirts and ruined it. She brought the interpreter with her so he could beg me on her behalf not to fire her. I had the interpreter tell her, "Hey, I understand mistakes happen," in whatever way he thought best. I gave her the shirt to take home for her family and she started to cry all over again. I had my interpreter escort her out to Baba at the end of the day so Baba would not think she was stealing my shirt.

When she came to work another morning, we couldn't miss the fact that Zermina had been crying. We asked what was wrong and she told us her young two year-old son had gotten into an open sewer and was very sick. Open sewers are very common. Right outside our Kabul house, the sewage ran in an unprotected ditch. Zermina was distraught as she could not afford a doctor, leaving her no option. Her mother told her that even though her boy was dying that she would be ok since she still had three other children.

We immediately had my interpreter take her home and take her son to the hospital, giving her money to pay the bill. The doctor sent a message back thanking us for saving the boy's life, noting that if it had been one more day, the boy would have died. A few days later Zermina brought her son to work so we could all meet the boy we saved. He was a happy healthy chubby cheeked 1½ year old little boy with sparkling mischievous eyes, along with her young daughter, approximately 10 years-old with pretty green eyes and dark shoulder length hair to watch him.

Zermina's Children (Copyright © Alan Buffard used with permission)

I tried teaching both Zermina and Safi about things I liked to eat in hopes of getting a little variety in our daily meals. One day when Zermina told me her mother had an apple tree, I suggested we make an apple pie. They had never ever seen an apple pie before, so since neither of them had a clue about apple pie, I emailed my wife and asked her to send me a recipe for it.

I had Zermina bring apples from home and the three of us went to work making a good old American apple pie. I wanted to give them a personalized taste of America. One question they asked me was why do you put a "lid" (crust) on the pie? I had no reason except we have always done it that way.

Surprisingly, the pie turned out OK. After having a piece with our next meal, I gave them the rest of it to take home. Who knows? That might have been the first home-made American apple pie in Afghanistan.

First Apple Pie

Zermina once asked me if she could have our empty plastic bottles. I assumed she sold them for money to be recycled. Naïve American! I found out later she was actually burning them in her stove at home for heat. I cringed at the thought of all the toxic gases she and her family were inhaling just to stay warm.

When it came time for me to finally leave Afghanistan, Zermina cried. I know she wanted to hug me but unfortunately we also both knew this was not permitted.

SHAMS, MY AFGHAN INTERPRETER

My Afghan interpreter was a young college man who could speak English as he continued taking English classes in the evenings. Shams was slightly built at 5 ½ feet tall with short black hair and a short-cropped beard. He was nice looking with a thin nose on his square face with deep set dark eyes and a forever smile on his face. He wore the traditional clean-just-pressed long white Afghan shirt over black baggy pants and sandals every day. I believe Shams salary represented the main income for his family.

In the evenings when he would come back to our house after English class, I would help him with English and he would help me with Dari. I always had Shams, who spoke both Afghan languages, and a PSD guard who spoke Arabic with me, as many of the business owners are educated in Arabic, so my PSD guard was an added bonus.

Shams came in one day so excited to show us his ink dyed finger signifying he got to vote! This was a risky privilege as if seen by the Taliban, they would cut his finger off.

As I mentioned before, Shams also drove one of the cars when we went out on missions. He would also frequently go out to the various marketplaces and get me prices on materials and equipment for bids on construction projects. This was a big help to me in my work, not to mention being a potential literal life-saver. He also stopped at the bread shop on the corner a couple times every day to get the flat bread for our meals. He was a young civilian, not military, therefore never carried a weapon.

Shams lived in a little room next to my office all week except Fridays, the day each week he would go home to be with his family. He and I would have discussions about his Islamic faith and my Christian beliefs. We enjoyed each other's company.

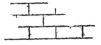

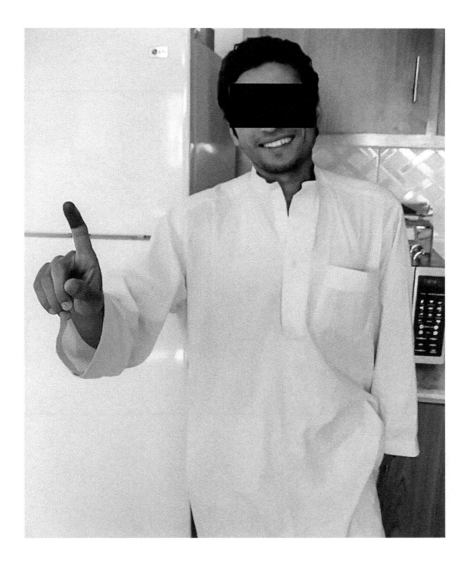

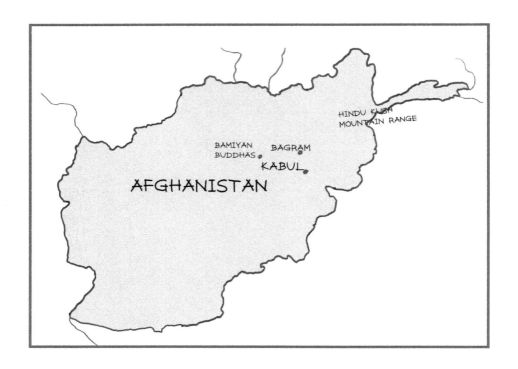

CHAPTER 5

Kabul House Visitors

*"It is foolish and wrong to mourn the men who died.
Rather, we should thank GOD such men lived."*
—General George S. Patton

At Kabul House, I often had a few distinguished friends stop by for afternoon tea. My guests were sometimes Afghan military generals and sometimes Afghan princes. All of them were quite interesting and our conversations were always entertaining.

THE AFGHAN GENERAL

Our company had arranged for the same Afghan General that walked me through customs upon arrival at the airport, to be our company security advisor. He gave us briefings of Taliban threat levels, was the liaison between us and the Afghan government for our jobs, facilitated obtaining Afghan entry visas as needed for our company and helped recommend contractors and material supply companies. He came to Kabul House several times a week to eat both lunch and dinner with us.

The first time he came to our home for an introductory visit, I was sitting on the couch with my legs crossed and the bottom of my shoe facing toward him. One of my Lebanese bodyguards kept signaling me from across the room, looking a bit upset. I couldn't understand what he was signaling me about. He finally came over to tell me to put my foot down.

I later learned that showing the bottom of your shoe to someone is really rude in Afghanistan and in some situations could get your head cut off. It soon became obvious that cutting off someone's head was the solution to most of the problems in this part of the world. I couldn't believe that displaying the bottom of one's shoe was actually a beheading offence, but I decided it was best to comply just in case. It sounded like my life might depend on learning these traditions, so I started taking them pretty seriously. I felt this was my first warning, I needed to learn their ways.

Just before the next General's visit, my security guard told me it was expected of me to drink alcohol with the General. I explained to my well-intentioned guard that I don't drink alcohol, but I have no problem with people who do. He told me this could cause big problems with the General and that refusing a drink might end up badly.

"Please just drink the alcohol. What difference can it make?" he pleaded. In spite of his warning, I let him know I would not start compromising my principles and that I would just accept whatever consequences that might entail.

The day finally arrived and as the General was being served alcohol, he asked me, "aren't you having a drink?" I told the General I didn't drink alcohol. My bodyguards looked very nervous as the General got up from his chair and came towards me. I can't explain how relieved I was when he gave me a big hug and told me I was a better Muslim than he was.

"I drink to forget all the people I have killed," he admitted with a sad face.

I glanced over at my security guards and saw a sigh of relief on their faces as they removed their hands from their side arms.

The General and his bodyguard were both great at playing an ancient guitar he always brought with him. He proudly told me this guitar dated back to the days of Genghis Khan. After dinner we would often sit around and visit while listening to him play. It was quite soothing to listen to the pleasant ancient music this man could make with his guitar, especially considering we were sitting smack dab in the middle of a war-torn nation.

The General and I

As my security advisor, the general taught me valuable techniques I needed to follow when performing everyday tasks in this high-risk war zone. Here, simply going out for bread might cost you your life.

Perhaps his biggest challenge was educating a naïve civilian like me about military realities, norms of the Muslim society, Middle East culture and the proper way of doing things in that part of the world, such as not showing the bottom of your shoe. He made me understand that doing things the wrong way could cost me my life. He instilled in me the need to become knowledgeable about Muslim beliefs and customs. "Ignorance of the customs here can get you killed," he often warned me.

One very important concept I had to adopt was the generally accepted belief that when anything went wrong, it was purely God's plan – period! The Afghans used the term "Inshallah" constantly, and it became engrained in my vocabulary. It means "It is God's will," meaning the Afghans were not responsible for anything because "Inshallah."

The General and I would talk about hunting a lot and he said someday he would take me up to Marzar-e-Sharif in Northern Afghanistan to go bird hunting. I said I would like that and mentioned I'd also like to see the famous Blue Mosque in Marzar-e-Sharif. He seemed pleasantly surprised that I knew about that Mosque. The General and the bodyguards got a kick out of kidding around with me, even suggesting that when we got up to Marzar-e-Sharif, they would sell me to the Taliban or hunt me instead of hunting birds. Run, Mr. Rich, Run.

I discussed my possible hunting trips with U.S. military personnel, who warned me, "No, you do not go up in the mountains hunting or anything else. They are full of land mines, left from the Russians." That put a halt on my Afghan hunting trips.

THE AFGHAN PRINCE

An Afghan Prince was a frequent guest at our house for dinner and would sometimes invite me to lunch at his home. Being educated abroad, he was quite intelligent and knowledgeable on a wide variety of subjects. After attending college in the U.S. where he majored in business and economics, the Prince returned to his native Afghanistan as an entrepreneur and established several successful businesses, some being construction companies.

"With my education and American connections, I could have worked abroad and made lots of money," he once told me with a sigh. "But I felt I needed to return here because I really want to do my part in making our country a better place."

I really had to admire that.

Doing charitable work was high on the Prince's priority list. He had been instrumental in building hundreds of homes and several Mosques for the poor across the country. Being a staunch supporter of education, he supplied materials to thousands of students.

I recall a rather insightful conversation I was having one afternoon with him. One comment I enjoyed from him was, "Do you know what Americans and Afghans have in common?" I really couldn't think of anything. He said, "The Afghans have beat the British in three wars, you Americans have only beat them in two wars. Afghanistan is where Empires come to die. As a nation, we have never been conquered," the prince was proud to point out. "Never."

When I told this comment to a Brit, he told me the British felt they lost the American revolutionary war to the French, not to the Americans. Hmmm ... I guess it depends on who's writing the history.

With the Prince's wisdom and experience combined with my studies and interest in history, we had many hours of stimulating conversation. The Prince's ancestors provided him a blood line linkage to most of the major tribes in Afghanistan through a few hundred marriages spread across the past century. Being a descendant of Afghan royalty, his stories gave me an understanding of Muslim and Afghan evolution that spanned centuries.

It was through the Prince that I came to understand that without tribal unification and education, there will be no economic development or social cohesiveness of any real substance in Afghanistan.

CAR BOMB ATTACK, KABUL

Unfortunately, car bomb attacks have gotten to be a fairly common occurrence in many parts of the Middle East, and Afghanistan is no exception.

One afternoon as I was sitting in our front yard at Kabul House sipping Turkish coffee with my Afghan General friend, a suicide car bomb exploded a few hundred yards away. It killed 17 and injured another 90+.

The General had just finished telling me how safe I would be at Kabul House because of the 5,000 soldiers he was bringing down from the north. He also told me he would be stationing a few hundred soldiers just a couple miles away and would have five helicopter gunships flying back and forth over all the neighborhoods in our part of the city.

The bomb exploded with enough shockwave to cause the ground to roll up and down and enough power to engulf me and the General in a smothering heat wave, blasting all the windows inward into the house. The returning shockwave, like an atomic bomb blast, sucked the doors off their hinges into the front yard. I gazed upward and saw what looked like a small atomic bomb mushroom cloud. I just stood there in shock. The General's only reaction when he saw the fear in my eyes was to grin and calmly say, "What, Mr. Rich, you are still alive aren't you?"

His laughter only made me wonder how these people lived like this year after year. It was just plain lucky no one in our house was hurt. Then a re-alization struck. It was all about luck! Simply being in the wrong place at the wrong time when one of these bombs explodes determines your fate. I agreed with my Lebanese guards that it's our faith that carries us through these experiences. Laughingly, they would remind me that if the worst did happen and we were killed, at least we'd all be "eating lamb in Paradise."

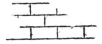

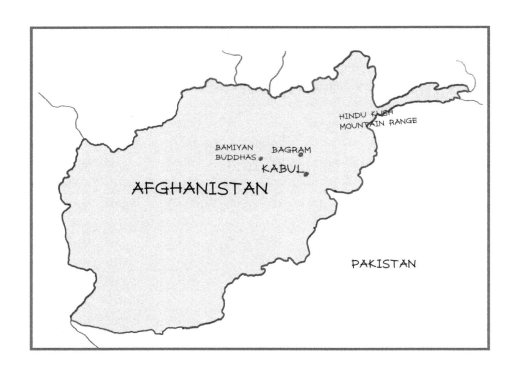

CHAPTER 6

Massive Culture Shock

"You don't live in a world all your own. Your brothers are here, too."
—Albert Schweitzer

While living at Kabul House, I got an "up close and personal" look at Muslims for the first time in my life, since all the Afghans living there and visiting us were Muslims. My Afghan interpreter read the Koran to our Afghan gatekeeper and prayed every morning in his room next to my office. He also read the Koran to our Afghan guards at lunch time every day. Remember, 80% of Afghans cannot read or write.

UNDERSTANDING AFGHAN AND MUSLIM CULTURE

Around 4:00 AM every morning, I woke up to morning prayer being broadcast over loud speakers from a couple different nearby Mosques. Then I would hear the call to prayer four more times each day and evening.

I learned to understand the level of devotion the Muslims openly display each and every day of their lives. While some of us may not agree with or understand their religious beliefs, we cannot mistake their dedication.

Our Afghan cook at Kabul House had a brother living down the street who killed his neighbor in a fierce argument. In order to make peace among the tribes and the two families involved in the tragedy, the man who committed the murder agreed to give his 11 and 13-year-old daughters to the men of the other tribe and everything would be forgiven. It was an old Pashtun Swara Law that a girl is given to a tribe as payment for a crime committed by her male relatives. Supposedly it is officially banned but still happens. That settled the debt and everything was "OK."

It became apparent to me that war has been a way of life for Afghans for centuries, not only fighting other countries trying to take them over, but also fighting amongst themselves between their tribes. During the time I was in Afghanistan, I heard the average lifespan of Afghans was 47 years. The ongoing devastation of Afghanistan was a huge contributing factor to that statistic. It was definitely a different culture than I was used to. I had a lot to learn about their traditions, tribes and the local fighters to keep myself out of trouble.

The Mujahedeen was a faction of Afghan fighters. The philosophy of the Mujahedeen when going into battle is that they cannot possibly lose, even if they are killed. Those who survive and defeat the enemy are the victors. If they die in battle, they automatically go to Paradise. Therefore, everyone comes out a winner and no one loses. I call that an Afghan "Win-Win".

How do you defeat a people with a belief like that? They will fight to the death and never surrender because they believe they will reap their ultimate reward regardless of the outcome. In their minds, they cannot lose. So, if you are looking for logic in the way things work in Afghanistan, you are not going to find it. The Greeks, the Brits, the Russians, and many others learned this the hard way. As I was told by the Afghan Prince, "Afghanistan is where empires come to die."

After a period of time and some near misses with death, I gradually began to adopt a similar attitude. If I survive, I get to live and if I get killed I go to heaven. Either way I am a winner.

GETTING USED TO AFGHAN CUSTOMS

Picture mud huts with no heat, no running water, no sewer systems, and generally little to no electricity, and you'll have a picture of how poor the country is in general. Even toilet paper is a luxury in Afghanistan; I carried my own everywhere.

Mud Huts (Copyright © Jim Ellis used with permission)

Another thing that became obvious to me about Middle East cultures while there, was the lack of significance they gave to last names. It wasn't hard to catch on to this since they immediately started calling me Mr. Rich instead of Mr. Walton. This fit right in with the feeling their society was stuck back in the biblical era. No one in the Bible has a last name.

I learned that many Afghan people simply made up last names for themselves to appease the westerners who basically demanded everyone needed to have both a first and a last name for legal identification purposes. It's very commonplace in that part of the world to have family members with different last names. Everyone was free to pick their own.

Western governments were also demanding to know each person's date of birth. Most Afghans did not know their birthdates. Their parents never kept track, so why did they need to know their date of birth? Afghans had no other choice than to simply make one up, just like they did with their last names. They would take a guess at how old they were and that determined the year part of the date. But what about the month and day? Based on my personal observation, a huge percentage of the population was supposedly born on January 1st.

Despite the Afghans' attitude toward such things, there was a huge downside to this 'no last name – no date of birth' scenario. When it comes to doing frivolous stuff like background checks for immigrants, the whole concept of vetting gets flushed down the toilet.

TALIBAN: THE INSIDE SCOOP

To truly understand what I was dealing with in Afghanistan, you must first understand who the Taliban are. Many believe the Taliban to be a faction or terrorists indigenous to Afghanistan, but this is not true. Most Taliban are Pashtun tribesmen from southern Afghanistan and northwestern Pakistan.

The word Taliban is a plural Pashto term meaning "students." The Taliban insurgency emerged in 1994 as one of the prominent factions in the Afghan Civil War, largely consisting of students from educational institutions in Pakistan that taught Islamic theology and religious law. The insurgency spread throughout most of Afghanistan, sequestering power from warlords and over-throwing and driving the Russians out, and the Taliban ruled Afghanistan from 1996 to 2001, enforcing a strict interpretation of Sharia, or Islamic law. I believe many of the Taliban are misdirected Afghans who believe they are simply preserving their way of life in accordance with the Koran and Allah.

The Taliban established the Islamic Emirate of Afghanistan in 1996 and the Afghan capital transferred to Kandahar. The Taliban held control of most of the country until being overthrown by the American-led invasion of Afghanistan in December 2001 following the September 11 attacks in the U.S.A.

I was told by local Afghans to look at the shirt-tails of the Afghan people and if the shirttail had square corners, there was a good chance they were Taliban. If the shirttail had rounded corners they were not. After that, I always looked at the Afghan shirttails.

WOMEN OF AFGHANISTAN

We've all heard stories about women being considered second-class citizens, however, the impact of seeing this in real life was shocking and sad.

In cities such as Kabul, many women are free to seek education and work. Some are even in relatively high positions in both the public sector and government, but that is not the case in most of the country.

While part of the Afghan society is still very abusive to women, the Taliban take it to the extreme. Specifically targeted by the Taliban are schools daring to educate Afghan girls. Members of the Taliban would throw acid in the faces of young girls who attended school as their way of preventing the education of women.

School - No Girls

Also, besides Afghan men having multiple wives, they can legally have one-year marriages. The bottom line is that Afghan men can take "temporary" wives, then terminate all obligations when these marriages end after a year. Even worse is being a divorced or unwed female with a baby. Considered by Afghan men not fit to marry, these women have no hope, no way to provide for themselves and no possibility for a man to provide for them.

This became even more real during one of my afternoon tea sessions with my good friend, the Afghan General. I was singing the blues about how lonely it was to be away from my wife for so long. Big mistake to mention that to the General.

"No problem, Mr. Rich," he bellowed. "I can fix you up with a wife for one year. When year is up…Poof! Like it never happened. I'm sure your wife will not mind." I told him I was not interested because I feared my wife more than the Taliban. He was as stunned with my answer as I was by his offer.

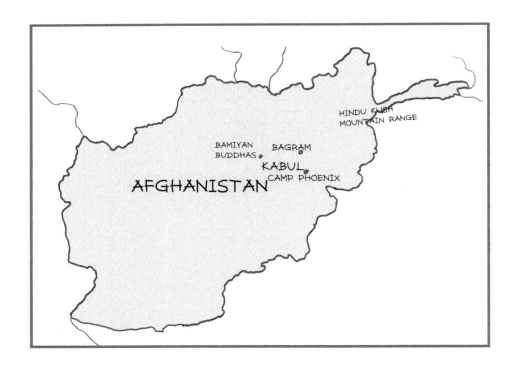

CHAPTER 7

Dangerous Working Conditions

"Courage comes by being brave; fear comes by holding back"
—Publius Syrus

Throughout the day and night those of us living at Kabul House could hear explosions in our own neighborhood and from other parts of the city. My Lebanese friends were so used to it they could tell by the sound exactly what kind of explosives were being used on every strike. They tried schooling me in this skill, but I never seemed to quite get it. When I realized they had been going through this since the age of 10, I didn't feel quite so stupid - just very, very grateful for growing up in America.

We were sitting together when one explosion took place.

"Hey, that was a 188 rocket!" I stated with authority.

Throwing up their hands in mock frustration, they grinned, "Wrong again, Mr. Rich. That was just a 170."

It was obvious they couldn't believe I still didn't know the difference by sound.

Looking back, I'm amazed how complacent I had become with the frequent incidents of the Taliban or terrorist wannabes driving around town in little pick-up trucks shooting at government buildings, businesses and people's houses. The words, "Welcome to Afghanistan, Mr. Rich," kept running through my head in a sarcastic tone.

When a bread shop down the street from my house was blown up, I admit it was very disturbing to me, while most around me just seemed to see it as a bothersome inconvenience. Many times before and after every explosion you could hear a crowd of local people yelling and chanting "Allah Akbar." Translated into English, this means "God is great." I never did get used to their practice of praising and celebrating death and destruction. Every time I heard someone shout "Allah Akbar" I wondered if there was going to be an explosion.

Living in Afghanistan, there is one thing pretty much always on your mind: your number could come up at any time, day or night, no matter where you are or what you are doing.

LIFE-THREATENING POSTAL RUNS - GETTING THE MAIL

Normal tasks even as simple as getting the mail can involve a huge risk factor in Afghanistan. While I lived at Kabul House, since there is no local mail service from home to home in Afghanistan, we had to drive an hour or so to Camp Phoenix, a US Army base, where I had to complete a class on postal regulations to receive a special ID card, which I had to show every time we went to pick up our mail.

Needless to say, going to Camp Phoenix was not just your garden variety run to the Post Office. In order to make a simple mail run, we would have to load up the vehicles with the security guards, guns and water just like any other mission. All the way to Camp Phoenix, we faced the possibility of rocket attacks, roadside bombs, suicide bombers and sniper fire.

Camp Phoenix Post Office (Copyright © Jim Ellis used with permission)

Because of all the danger, we didn't go out to get the mail every day. We never got into a set routine when we ventured outside the house for anything. Even though we liked getting letters and packages from home, it wasn't worth putting our lives at risk as part of a daily routine.

MORE BOMBS AND ROCKETS

There were all kinds of bombs and rockets that could kill you in Afghanistan wherever you were. Incoming rockets and mortar fire were the most common, but the Taliban had many other tricks up their sleeves.

Terrorists come up with hundreds of creative ways to conceal bombs. There were bombs hidden in wooden carts, wheelbarrows, and in and under dead animals on the side of the road. They even resorted to shoving bombs up the asses of donkeys that were alive and walking around.

Bicycle bombs were also being used. So, bikes on the bases were not allowed to be parked by the areas where a lot of people assembled. You would not see them near gyms, dining halls, chapels or any structure of a community nature.

And then of course you had the suicide bombers who came in many forms. It was not that unusual for a Taliban terrorist to drive up to his target on his scooter and blow himself up, taking nearby people with him. It's amazing how many zealots find honor in dying this way.

And then there were the commonplace car bombs which could be left in vehicles parked on the side of the road or driven into a crowd by a suicidal maniac. Devastating IED's could be placed almost anywhere.

The craftier terrorists might even attach a magnetic bomb to a person's vehicle when they weren't looking. When entering military bases and arriving back at our home, we would have to have our vehicle checked for these magnetically attached devices. That would always creep me out - sitting in the vehicle while it was being checked, wondering if a bomb was about to explode with us inside.

EVEN A HAIRCUT COULD BE A CLOSE CALL

Going out in public for simple things like a haircut can be a major undertaking in a war zone like Kabul. My PSD guys considered it too dangerous to take me to a local Barber shop in the city. It would have been too hard to secure a barber shop and having me sit in a vulnerable place for any extended time was too great a risk. When I needed a haircut, my Lebanese body guards would have to go get a barber that they could trust and bring him back to my house to cut my hair. I had fond memories of being back in Portland where there was no need to worry about snipers or suicide bombers when I stepped out to go to the barber shop.

I thought it strange that my bodyguards would stand nearby with their hands on their pistols as I got my hair cut in the relative safety of the house. My interpreter would stand by my side and made sure the barber understood how I wanted my hair cut. When the barber finished my haircut, he asked if I wanted him to shave my neck around the bottom of my beard. After I said OK, he pulled out a straight razor.

I almost freaked out and asked my bodyguards, "what if he tries to cut my throat?"

"No problem, Mr. Rich," one of them grinned. "If he slits your throat, I kill him."

"But wait a minute," I said. "If you kill him, I'll still bleed to death."

My bodyguards laughed and said "Oh yah! ... But then, Mr. Rich, You'll be eating lamb in paradise."

I told the Barber to put away the straight razor, Mr. Rich didn't need a neck shave, realizing that something as mundane as getting a haircut in my own home could get me killed.

GROCERY SHOPPING, KABUL STYLE

Since even everyday trips to the grocery story were considered security risks and involved all the precautions that entailed, my Afghan interpreter would go out and buy groceries when they were needed. I did most of my own shopping whenever I was at a military base that had a PX.

Due to the occasional longing for some American food, I would occasionally have my security detail take me to a particular store in Kabul that sold western food. Such shopping excursions were not to be taken lightly. My company had never had anyone killed in Iraq or Afghanistan and they didn't want to ruin that record with me being killed going to the store for treats. My Lebanese PSD guys and a few Afghan security guards carrying Ak-47s had to accompany me to the store.

As always, we had to take two cars in case my car was disabled by an attack or mechanical failure. That way they could transfer me to the other car and get me out of harm's way. After pulling up to the store, my Afghan security guards would surround the car before I got out.

Then my Lebanese PSD would go in the store and check for possible danger. Only then would the Lebanese escort me into the store with their 9 mm Beretta hand guns tucked in plain site into their belts. They followed me as I shopped. When I was done, they would keep me back from the cashier and not let me wait in line. They would clear out a space by moving people back and have me then come up to the cashier to pay for my food and walk me quickly out to the car. It was the same routine we used when I went to meetings in the city. The company needed to do this to protect me from getting killed or kidnapped.

IT'S NOT ONLY THE TRAFFIC THAT'S KILLING ME

Whenever I would go to meet with Afghan businessmen in the city, my Afghan guards would first get out of their car and go into the building to sweep the area inside. When they were reasonably sure it was safe, they would come back out to escort me inside for the meeting.

I felt like a foreign dignitary one might see in the movies as they surrounded the car with their weapons pointing in all directions. But there was more. Not trusting my fate to the surveillance done by the Afghan guards, my trusty Lebanese PSD guys went inside the building themselves to clear the area and see where we would be meeting.

Only after my Lebanese bodyguards were OK with the surroundings would they give a signal, help me out of the car, push my head down and surround me as we rushed into the building. At first I felt I had to apologize for all the fuss to the local businessmen, but they all took it in as part of doing business with an American.

Once inside, the Lebanese would select where I was to sit. It was always out of harm's way, safe from sniper fire through the windows or hallways. We were all offered food and tea but my body guards would always decline and stand by my side with their hands on their pistols.

During the meeting, my Afghan guards would stay outside guarding the vehicles and the doorway to the building. When I was ready to leave, the guards would quickly survey the area and give me the "all clear" signal. Then I would make a mad rush for the car and jump inside.

When going through congested areas, my PSD buddies warned me of the possibility of being taken by the Afghan police. I had actually heard stories of them putting unlucky foreigners in jail until a ransom was paid. I had even been told that some members of the Afghan police force acted as police by day and Taliban by night.

When stopped by the police, my PSD bodyguards would tell them I was a business man from Nuristan (Nuristan is in Northern Afghanistan where I resembled the local people with blue eyes which were descendants of Alexander the Great.) Fortunately, the police wisely backed off because of my body guards and the guns they were toting.

5TH WORLD – BIBLICAL TIMES, IN JESUS' DAY

As we ventured out into the desert to check out construction sites in remote areas, it looked to me as if things probably had not changed in 2,000 years or more. In my brief visit to Iraq, I saw it to be the third world country I had heard it was. If Iraq is third world, then Afghanistan is fifth world. It's just like biblical times, in Jesus' day. The many years of endless war and the lack of education had taken its toll on Afghanistan.

Building Materials Delivery? (Copyright © Jim Ellis used with permission)

Alongside the road, I would often see women and children asking for food and water, but we could not risk stopping to help them. My body guards warned me that some of these seemingly innocent kids might actually be sitting on an IED (Improvised Explosive Device) without knowing it, just waiting for an unsuspecting American victim to happen by.

On construction jobs in remote areas with a reputation for Taliban attacks, only managers and laborers of the local tribes were able to work. When I interviewed Afghans in Kabul qualified to be job site managers, they would always ask the location of the job site. If the job site was remote and in an area more prone to attacks than average, 95% of the Afghans in Kabul would say, "No way, you could not pay me enough to work in that area." This was my first lesson of Tribal Afghanistan. I would say, "Wait a minute, this is your country. Why aren't you willing to go there?" Needless to say, the only answers I got back were blank stares.

CONCRETE – WE CERTIFY OUR OWN!

I faced a lot of challenges when it came to acquiring construction materials. It was usually tough to find suppliers whose materials were in compliance with the standards required by US government organizations. One commodity that was particularly problematic was concrete.

Afghanistan Concrete Plant

There were concrete plants in the larger cities, but they were not viable for remote projects where the concrete trucks would have to drive a long distance. For large projects the alternative is what we called batch plants, i.e. portable plants that can be set up on the construction site for making concrete. The downside of these batch plants is that they made attractive targets for Taliban rockets and mortars.

Out in the countryside, concrete was made in small mixers by local Afghan workers, and in many very remote areas, it was mixed on the ground with nothing but a shovel.

One of the most important standards concerning concrete was the strength of the product, which can vary greatly depending on the raw materials used in the mixture. I always got suspicious when I heard the standard reply to my inquiries, "No problem, Mr. Rich," they'd usually say, "We test and certify our own concrete."

While they had "testing labs," those could be anything from a mud hut out back to a more modern lab with British-made testing equipment. How could I be sure the end product is what they say it is? To be certain, I had to find independent labs to do testing. Keep in mind the Afghans communicate amongst themselves, so collusion happens. I could really see the value of the four principles I had learned when I started: lie to you, cheat you, steal from you and kill you.

Working with Concrete Crew

This brought cold calling into a whole new perspective for me. I never knew how I'd be greeted when I pulled onto someone's property to find out about their concrete products. Would I be welcomed as a prospective customer or ignored as a pesky foreigner, or even shot at? My Lebanese bodyguards were always on edge and wouldn't let me get out of the car until they had a chance to check out the area.

Some business owners would talk to me and others would not. I also knew there was a strong possibility of being fed a pack of lies when I asked about quality and final price. Yet another business challenge.

Like many building material suppliers in Afghanistan, the concrete vendors were experts at misrepresentation. Like any good construction manager, I'd get competitive bids on goods and services whenever possible. I was dumbfounded more than once when I'd be comparing supposed competitors submitting bids. On one particular job where I was getting bids from three different suppliers, I broke down in laughter when all three presented brochures that were virtually identical except for the company name. Photos of the equipment each claimed to have were identical. This was a scam taken to a level I had not seen before. I had to laugh.

"Only in Afghanistan!"

Whenever I caught one of the shady suppliers or sub-contractors in a lie, the scenario was always the same. The crafty individual would just look at me with a smile and say, "Oh, Mr. Rich, mine is the REAL brochure!"

Or he would throw his hands up in the air and say, "You caught me, Mr. Rich." They'd laugh as if to say, "Would you expect anything else from me?"

All this dishonesty made my job much harder than it should have been. Whenever I got a quote on materials, I not only had to compare quality and price, but I also physically visited each supplier's facility to make sure it was real and not just a fictitious address in the middle of nowhere.

GOING TO SEE JESUS

One day I had to schedule a meeting out at Bagram Air Field a few hours outside of Kabul. The road going to Bagram was a hot bed for sniper attacks and IED's. I selected Wednesday for the trip. As we were making our way out to the base, we passed the charred carcass of a car that had been blown up on Tuesday. I heard about it on the morning news and felt a little ill as I remembered the reporter saying that five people had been killed with a car bomb on this very road.

Thursday, the following day, another news report showed several more people being killed with a bomb in almost the same place. Now I did feel sick. The Lebanese guys kidded me about making a good choice on the day I picked to make the visit to the base. In spite of their joking around, I cringed at the thought that if I had chosen to make the trip a day earlier or a day later, I could have cost everyone their lives. My Lebanese friends shrugged it off as just another day at the office.

The following week, I told one of the Lebanese we were going to have to go back out to Bagram again and I asked him how dangerous it was going to be. His reply was, "Well Mr. Rich, I think you're going to see Jesus today."

I realized I was getting a little too calloused when I jokingly told the Lebanese guys that maybe I should email my wife and let her know, "I might be seeing Jesus today."

The guys just laughed at my new-found attitude. This soon became their standard way of letting me know how dangerous any given trip would be. If it might be time "to see Jesus," I knew I could be killed.

Nomads in Tents (Copyright © Jim Ellis used with permission)

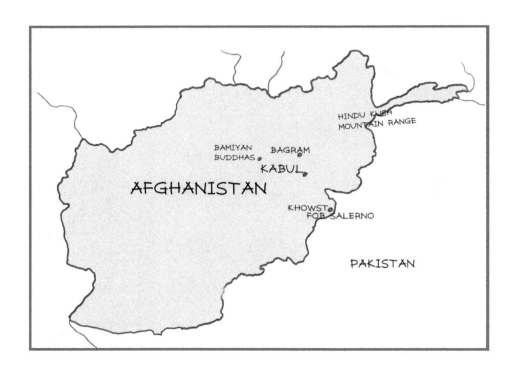

CHAPTER 8

Home and Back Again

"I know the price of success; dedication, hard work and unremitting devotion to the things you want to see happen."
—Frank Lloyd Wright

The job I had been hired for ended after four months. On my way home, my first layover from Afghanistan was Dubai. The Dubai Airport has a two-story indoor international mall to stroll through during long layovers. I have never seen anything like it at an airport. Extravagant, large, duty free shopping included everything from expensive clothing, accessories, candy and liquor to super expensive jewelry kiosks, gold, and silver, plus displays of luxurious cars. When we landed on that trip, I could hardly see the runway because of a sand storm.

At my next layover in Zurich, Switzerland, while clearing customs, the authorities pulled me aside for a more thorough personal search. I assumed it was because of my new look and my passport showing all the Middle East countries I had been to. They escorted me to a closed down security checkpoint on another floor, having me strip down to my t-shirt and pants and empty everything out of my pockets and backpack. They patted me down, then put all my clothes, shoes, belt, hat, everything out of my pockets and backpack through an x-ray machine. They told me that because I was good-natured about this search they would let me be one of the first to board my plane. Back at my gate, before anyone else was allowed to board, I heard it: "Mr. Walton please board the plane." As I passed everyone to be the first to go through the gate, it was such an awesome feeling. I am sure the way people looked at me, they had to wonder, who is this guy with the scraggly beard, little brown pakol hat, middle eastern beige vest and slacks topped off with a plaid Afghan scarf. Didn't they know it was Mr. Rich?

So far, going half way around the world for a job in a war zone was the hardest thing I have ever done, but also the most rewarding. When soldiers come home and talk about their deployments, I can now relate. It's hard to replace the constant living on the edge and adrenaline rush of danger.

One thing that took me by surprise were the flashbacks triggered by certain events. My wife and I decided to go see the movie *The Hurt Locker*. The opening scenes of a car and roadside bomb exploding sent me immediately back to Afghanistan and the car bomb explosion I had experienced at our home in Kabul. All the fears and thoughts immediately ran through my mind and I felt like I was back in that moment, not knowing if I was going to live or die. I really don't remember much of the movie after that.

BACK TO THE DRAWING BOARD

Back home in my office working my Architectural Design business again, I sat at my desk, finding my mind wandering back to Afghanistan and wondering if that was it. I wanted to be back.

After working overseas, I realized I needed more computer knowledge besides Architectural AutoCAD. I took classes to invest in myself and better develop my *Outlook, Word, Excel, Power Point* and *Microsoft Project* skills. If the opportunity came to go back, I wanted to be more prepared.

Again, my wife came to my rescue with another connection through the United States Naval Academy Parents. We were referred to an Electrical Engineer working in Afghanistan who sent me to his company HR. Within two weeks, I was hired and packing again.

A SECOND TIME – BACK TO AFGHANISTAN

This new job took me to Tyndale Air Force Base in Panama, Florida, for a week of orientation and a full physical, including new shots, Anthrax and Small Pox, a new supply of Malaria pills, plus a sample of my DNA for my remains identification. That was a cheerful thought.

I was hired to be a Construction Manager for a private US company working in conjunction with the US Air Force in the reconstruction of Afghanistan. My job before was bidding the jobs to win the competitive contracts. This time under the direction of the US Air Force personnel, I would also be verifying that the construction contracts were being done correctly and on time.

The entry into Afghanistan was different with this new job. I had to go through former US Military installation Manas Air Force Base in Bishkek, Kyrgyzstan first. The guards at the Bishkek airport were intimidating in their Russian style uniforms. Not only did they make me nervous, my next challenge was luggage. My luggage did not arrive with me. Three giant duffel bags were lost. I had nothing going into Afghanistan. I lost all my personal stuff, clothes, toiletries, boots and flashlights. I had only the clothes I was wearing and my backpack with my computer and my malaria pills. What a way to start a new job 7,000 miles from home in a fifth world country. What kept going through my head? "Welcome to Afghanistan, Mr. Rich."

At Manas, I was issued government equipment to be deployed to a war zone, consisting of body amour (a helmet and bullet proof vest), severe winter clothes, a sleeping bag, gas mask and chemical suit. I did not have any of that stuff before. What the heck?

I spent a week with soldiers in-processing and being issued equipment, living in a tan colored canvas tent. It had a hard door on the front and was set up on a wooden floor with at least a dozen bunks inside. After that, I flew to Afghanistan on a military flight with military troops and other civilian contractors. Most of the contractors traveling with me were ex-military. My next challenge? Not knowing all the military acronyms, abbreviations, buzzwords, processes and way of doing things. I had lots to learn.

Not having luggage or understanding what was going on was a good start for me for my second time in Afghanistan. In addition, I was supposed to be assigned to Kandahar in the South, but once at Bagram Air Field that was cancelled. I couldn't believe it. I met my new boss. His first comment to me was "What am I going to do with you now?" I had no luggage, no extra clothes, not understanding the military way of things, and now, nowhere to go.

Finally, after several days, they decided to send me to Forward Operating Base (FOB) Salerno in the East on the Pakistan border. Several kind contractors gathered some clothes for me as they casually mentioned, "did you know the nickname for that base is Rocket City because of the constant rocket attacks?" Oh great! And I was off to Salerno on a C-130 military flight. My second Afghan adventure continues.

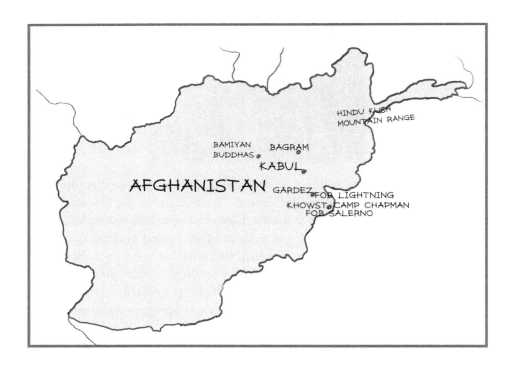

CHAPTER 9

FOB Salerno – Rocket City

*"It is not death that man should fear, he should fear
never beginning to live"*
—Marcus Aurelius

I was a civilian contractor assigned to work with the 577th Air Expeditionary Squadron known as *Prime Beef*. They assigned us contractors construction projects to manage and arranged helicopter flights to transport us to the projects. FOB Salerno was considered a HUB and from there I would travel to projects on smaller and more remote bases. The projects were U.S. military and Afghan Military projects generally under $750,000. FOB Salerno was in the same area as Camp Chapman in the movie *Zero Dark 30*, in the Khost province of Afghanistan.

ROCKET ATTACKS AT SALERNO – MISSED ME!

The living on Salerno was ok, except for the rocket attacks and poisonous snakes and spiders that could kill me. Plus, suicide bombers and Taliban attacks hit the base once in a while. All the meals and laundry were free. FOB Salerno, like all the other bases, except larger Bagram and Kandahar, was a "Black Out" base. All outside lights must be off at night, leaving the base pitch black for us to stumble around in the dark finding our way to latrines, other tents and buildings. No white flashlights, only green, red or blue lights were allowed. That made it harder for the Taliban to target us, as was not wearing the reflective vests required on the large bases. You had to be very careful walking around on a black out base. I know of a soldier that walked into some "C" wire (razer barbed wire) at night. He needed several stitches.

I flew to different bases a couple times a week with my back pack and sleeping bag, overseeing construction projects. While I worked at FOB Salerno, we took rocket hits at all hours of the day and night. Salerno was nicknamed "Rocket City" because of the frequency of rocket and mortar attacks. And of course, I had projects to oversee out at the far end of the base away from the safety of the bunkers.

We had standing orders to either stay in our office, which was a hardened structure, or run to a bunker if we were out in the open when we heard the "INCOMING, INCOMING" warning over the PA system, also referred to as the "Big Voice."

The best place to be when a rocket attack happened was inside the DFAC (Dining Facility). Not only was it a hardened structure, but we could eat and drink plus watch TV while waiting for the "all clear" signal, which could take several hours.

There were a few people killed by rockets when I was at FOB Salerno. One was a U.S. Army officer driving his Gator (4 wheel drive ATV) down the road on base when a rocket landed right on top of him. It's one thing to see a terrible incident like this in a war movie but quite another to have it happen right in your own back yard.

One day a rocket hit the building next to where I was sleeping. The rocket went right through the door into the room and blew up inside. Lucky there was no one in the room. Had there been, he or she certainly would have been killed. Actually, the guy assigned to that room had decided to go to bed late that night. It was only one time out of many during my tour when either I or someone I knew could easily have died but experienced only a near miss instead.

JUST NOT MY DAY – FOB SALERNO

While talking to a young soldier one day, he told me he had gone outside in the middle of the night to take a piss not long ago and a rocket exploded just a few feet away from him. The explosion embedded many small bomb fragments into his back. As he was recovering, his commanding officer told him he could go back home three months early because of his injury. That young soldier declined the offer to leave Afghanistan early.

"That day was just not my day," he said nonchalantly, "and I'm not quitting early." While others questioned his sanity, I admired him for his strong sense of patriotic duty.

How many times did I go outside in the middle of the night to take a leak and think about him and wonder if my number would be up before I zipped up my pants? Taking a piss could cost you your life there.

That young soldier told me he'd "be taking part of Afghanistan back home with him in the form of rocket fragments the doctors could not remove."

The rockets started coming in all the time. I often wondered if a rocket was going to hit the bunker and if the structure would hold up to the explosion. Throughout the bunker I could hear people cracking jokes and telling funny stories just to pass the time and take their minds off the unpleasantness of it all.

I have been in the latrine and many other places when I heard the dreaded "Incoming-Incoming" alert. One time I was working out in the gym. Forget a shower – head for the bunker!

My fellow gym rats and I fled quickly out the door. Since we had all come from the gym, everyone in the bunker with me was sweaty and stinky. The concrete bunker soon became like a steam bath due to the heat mixed with all the perspiration. Our clothes were drenched with sweat and the stench was getting pretty strong. We were all hoping this would be one of those attacks that would last for only 15-20 minutes, rather than the occasional 1-2 hour ordeal before the "all clear" signal. That type of shit could ruin your whole day!

Looking around, I'd see people of all ages, from the 18 year-old recruits to 60 year-old senior citizens like me, young soldiers, older officers, doctors, and laborers, for a brief period of time all getting along and trying to make the best of a bad situation. Nowhere else can I imagine such a diverse group of people getting along as if they were the best of friends. Once the "all clear" announced, everyone left the bunker and walked right back into the world the way things were before.

FOB LIGHTNING ATTACKS

One of the first remote bases I traveled to from FOB Salerno was FOB Lightning in Gardez, Paktia Province, in southeast Afghanistan. My job was to check and oversee the building of their dog kennel compound, used for housing military working dogs (drug and attack dogs) and a TERP Village (where Afghan interpreters would live and eat) just outside the wire – what we called a grey area. We were tearing down the old buildings, for sleeping, eating, offices, and laundry, and replacing with new buildings. When the US Army went to the village, they traveled in a group and carried guns. When I went, I went by myself, carrying my backpack and a smile.

The first time I visited COP Lightening, it was hot and I couldn't figure out why I was getting so tired just walking. I learned it was at 7,000 feet elevation – no wonder. I thought I was just getting old.

I was on my way to FOB Lightning one day when a suicide bomber blew himself up in the Afghan Bazaar on the base. This bazaar was between the base and the TERP Village. I had walked past that Bazaar many times and often stopped in to buy a few things I needed or interesting trinkets. After a string of incidents like this, I adopted a new motto: it's either your time to die or it isn't.

Military base Afghan Bazaar (Copyright © Jim Ellis used with permission)

Because FOB Lightning was in the mountains and continuous bad weather keeping helicopters at bay, I would quite often get stuck there for a week at a time. Sometimes the bad weather was Taliban attacks. I slept on a cot in a B-Hut (a plywood building in various sizes for sleeping in), generally by myself. Because Lightning was an old British base, the electricity was 220v instead of American 120v. I always needed my adapters for my electrical equipment to work. Only my cell phone could be charged on either.

One night sitting on the steps of the "B-Hut," the PA system suddenly began blaring "Sandman, Sandman." Soldiers were running all over the place with their IBA (battle gear) on and weapons. I asked a soldier running by me what Sandman meant. "Sir, I don't know what it means to you, but I got to go." On bases they had call signs that meant different things to everyone. I didn't know mine yet. Later I found out we were under a ground attack from Taliban. Flares shot into the sky lighting up the perimeter. Lots of fire going out, mortars or artillery guns. I didn't know where to go or what to do. All I could do was just sit listening and watch the flares and sky light up. The next morning everything was back to normal.

HELICOPTERS GONE CRAZY

I was waiting at the Helicopter Landing Zone (HLZ) at FOB Lightning with two U.S. Soldiers, when some ANA (Afghan National Army) helicopter pilots were being trained. We were standing on one landing pad across a small ravine from another landing pad being used for the training exercise. There was a helicopter trying to take off and the Afghan pilot was having some serious problems.

The chopper was bouncing up and down as he moved forward on the landing pad. All of a sudden, the chopper rolled off the landing pad and down into a ravine full of rocks. Soon we saw the rotor blades coming up out of the ravine and then the helicopter itself. As it got to the top of the ravine, it started flailing along the ground coming right for us. "Holy Shit!" We ran for our lives. No one was hurt, and when the pilot finally got the helicopter to the landing pad where we had been standing, he was able to take off. I was surprised the helicopter wheels didn't break off from hitting all the rocks in the ravine. It was a Russian helicopter so maybe they are built for that type of thing. Just one more weird event.

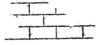

Inspecting top of a Storage Fuel Tank

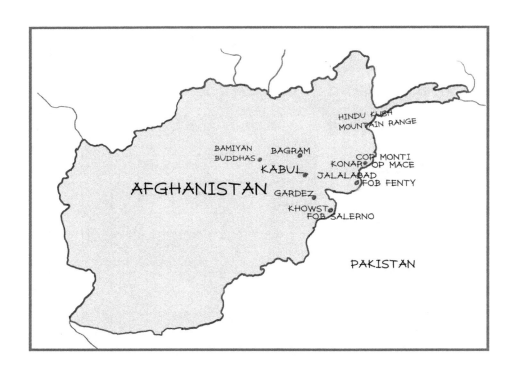

CHAPTER 10

From the Frying Pan into the Fire

"A great wind is blowing, and that gives you either imagination or a headache."

—Catherine the Great

Three months after I arrived in Afghanistan and moved to FOB Salerno, word came that my long lost duffel bags were finally found. I had just picked them up when my lead construction manager informed me I had to pack and move to Jalalabad by that night.

LEAVING SALERNO – VOILA, LOST BAGS APPEAR!

Packing consisted of things from my office including everything in my desk and bedroom, plus boxing up and mailing items I could not take on the plane. I was just getting used to Salerno, and I knew nothing about Jalalabad. "Here we go," I thought. Another adventure.

Flying from Salerno through the night, I arrived at the PAX (Bagram Air Terminal) to fly to Jalalabad. There were no flights to Jalalabad for days! I went from official to official, asking what I could do. What other modes of transportation were there? I needed to get to my next duty station.

I found there was another type of private airline called Stow Flights – small private planes that flew smaller crews to other bases. I found a flight going to Jalalabad. It was first come, first serve. I'd been in line for a while, when I learned there was a weight limit per person and I was well over that. I had to get creative and started asking guys around me that only had a back-pack if I could use their weight allowance to carry my bags. They said "Sure." So I had my bags spread out and it all got on the plane. The officials did not like me doing this, but their supervisor allowed it this one time.

ARRIVING IN JALALABAD – FOB FENTY AT JBAD

Arriving at the Jalalabad airport next to FOB Fenty at night was different. I had to walk across an active runway to get to where most of the living and sleeping buildings were. Being a black out base, I couldn't see and didn't know where to go. I had the lead construction manager's cell number only to not have any cell phone service available as they also shut the cell towers off at night. I walked around in the dark until I found the airport office with a land phone I could use. To my relief, he came and we walked to my office and sleeping quarters. Sometimes it seemed my whole day was just solving one roadblock after another.

ASSORTMENT OF MILITARY BASES

Like most countries in which foreign military personnel are deployed, there is a handful of different types of bases depending on size, strategic importance, proximity to population centers and the nature of each base's mission. During my four years in Afghanistan, I had occasion to visit bases of all types and sizes. In some brief research I did, I discovered at one time there were over 700 military bases scattered throughout Afghanistan at the peak of the military turmoil. To prepare for the project I was going to visit, so I would have a heads up of what equipment and materials were available, It was helpful to me to know the various designations and characteristics of the different base types.

Airfield – An Air Force base used by military for military aircraft.

Combat Outpost – COP – A small base which can contain between 40 and 150 service members and is usually placed in hostile locations.

Forward Operating Base – FOB – A base that is larger than a COP, but smaller than a full-function base. They tend to be located in less dangerous areas and offer "luxuries" such as varied meals and hot water.

Camp – A temporary military facility erected away from the major bases. The Afghan Army called some of their bases Camps and the U.S. Marines refer to all their bases as Camps. Camp Leatherneck, for example, is a huge military base.

Observation Point, aka Observation Post – OP – A small outpost built at a high elevation intended primarily for surveilling the surrounding countryside.

OBSERVATION POINT MACE

One typical cold December morning in 2011, I was sitting at my desk at FOB Fenty, located in the northeast of Afghanistan, near the Pakistan Border, when a U.S. Army Colonel came into our office. He talked to the Master Sergeant who then pointed at me. I wondered what I had done. The Colonel asked me if I could draw some buildings for him.

"No problem," I offered. "Let's just send them to my Air Force office in Bagram to have them done."

There's an official process back at the Bagram office I was supposed to use when creating drawings, and I complied with that most of the time. However, in a war zone environment, there are often special emergency situations where time is of the essence and people can't wait for all the red tape to be applied. I guess you could say in some cases, I sort of used my own brand of "duct tape" as a substitute for the official red tape. On this occasion, the Colonel told me he didn't have the time to go through all the red tape to get the buildings drawn up in AutoCAD by the people in Bagram. I could see the urgency in his face.

"Sure, I'll be glad to help you. What do you need"?

He told me he needed four buildings drawn up so they could get the materials ordered and flown up to OP Mace right away. There was a slight problem in that since the materials were going to be flown up by helicopter, so nothing could be over eight feet in length.

"No problem," I grinned at the challenge. "So when do you need them?"

"Tomorrow."

"WHAT!? Tomorrow?" I said, "You are kidding me, right? That's FOUR buildings!"

His gruff response told me all I needed to know. I assured him I would do my best and got busy on AutoCAD. I stayed up all night with help from lots of energy drinks and coffee. As I finished them the next day, I thought to myself that I was lucky all the caffeine had not given me a heart attack.

When the Colonel arrived in the morning, I gave him the drawings on a CD in a format that could be printed using just a regular copy machine. He thanked me profusely, knowing I had stayed up all night to finish his job, then immediately took off with CD in hand. I commented to the Master Sergeant that we were running out of energy drinks as I headed off to catch a nap.

A few days later, the Master Sergeant asked me to go out to the airfield and meet a C-130 military plane that was coming in. He said there was a package he needed to get from the plane. As I approached the C-130 on the tarmac, a guy came down the ramp and asked, "Are you Mr. Walton?" After I said yes, he handed me a few cases of energy drinks and said, "Complements of the Colonel, Mr. Walton."

I said thanks and when I got back to the office all the military guys were laughing because they knew what was going on. I put the energy drinks under my desk where they lasted for several weeks. As I always say, what goes around comes around.

Later, the Master Sergeant showed me a *Stars and Stripes* magazine article with photos showing the buildings I had drawn being built on top of a mountain at OP Mace. It was really cool to see the results of my work as part of that project.

UP ON THE ROOF

I was often called on to do sketches and detailed architectural drawings to help the Air Force and Army guys doing construction projects in the field. One such design was for a roof that would need to support heavy snow loads. I completed the drawing for one of the guys unofficially and didn't think anything more about it.

One day at FOB Fenty, a Lieutenant Colonel was visiting our office and using the computer next to mine. We talked about a few projects and he showed me a detailed drawing they had been using on several buildings. He asked me if I would be willing to make some changes on it for a specific site having some unique requirements. I had to chuckle when I saw the drawing.

"I drew this," I blurted out.

"Wow," he said. "No shit, your drawings have really helped us. And now I have a face and a name to go with so many drawings we used."

Construction Work at COP Monti

When the U.S. Army Captain in charge of COP Monti found out I had designed this extra heavy-duty roof for snow, he wanted me to design a stand-off roof for rocket attacks for the main building where most of his soldiers slept and worked. He told me I had to see something and led me to a soldier's room. He showed me where a Taliban rocket had gone through the roof and ran down a plywood wall, burning the plywood, and stuck in the floor by the soldier's head while he was lying in bed. The soldier looked at it and didn't know if he should move or not. He did finally get up, and the rocket never exploded. But because of this incident, the Captain wanted at least one place his soldiers could feel relatively safe from rocket attacks.

To get the process started, I had to measure the building so I could draw the existing building using AutoCAD. It was an old Russian building that was huge. Because of its size, it took me a few days with U.S. soldiers helping me measure the dimensions. It was nerve-racking for the soldiers because they didn't like being sitting ducks on the roof.

"Hey Mr. Walton, do you have to do this kind of stuff very often?" one of the soldiers asked.

"Of course," I responded, "it's my job."

He just shook his head and muttered, "With all due respect, Mr. Walton, you're frickin' nuts!"

Adhering to official procedure this time, I sent the drawings to the Air Force engineering department in Bagram. They designed a couple solutions which, when presented, were deemed too expensive and difficult to build, so the soldiers never got their rocket-proof roof.

COP MONTI UNDER ATTACK - KUNAR PROVINCE

One day I was flying out to COP Monti without a security detail and the outpost was under sniper attack, as it often was. COP Monti was located in Eastern Afghanistan by the Pakistan border, in the Kunar River Valley. We were in a civilian Huey Helicopter piloted by two South Africans. I was the only one in the chopper other than the pilots, who knew me because I was a 'frequent flier' with them. They told me they couldn't land because the base was under attack.

"But we will show them a little air presence," one of the pilots chuckled.

"What the hell does that mean?" I asked. "We have no guns on this chopper."

They laughed. "But the Taliban don't know that!"

We flew around the base a couple times looking like we were on a hunt for targets. That was crazy, but I have to admit it was fun.

We came back and landed the next day, and the soldiers there were laughing while talking about a story of a civilian helicopter flying around above them during a Taliban attack.

"No shit," I chimed in. "I was on that Helicopter!" We all had a big laugh.

Ancient British Outpost at COP Monti

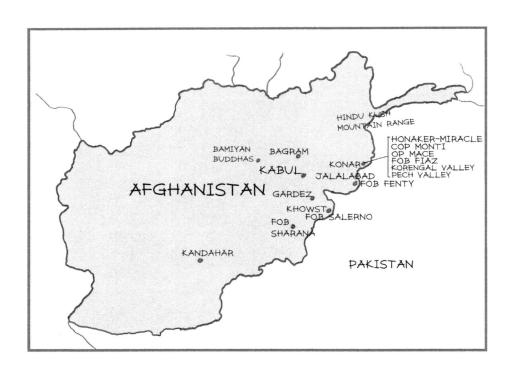

CHAPTER 11

Mr. Rich, the Cat with Nine Lives

"The measure of a man is the way he bears up under Misfortune"
—Plutarch

Throughout my time in Afghanistan, I was often referred to as the "Cat with Nine Lives" because of all the close calls I'd had. The soldiers and my co-workers would count down how many lives I had left. Starting with the Kabul House car bomb, I had lost count. Was number nine still out there waiting to strike me down? Several friendly "associates" jokingly told me they would let me know when I got down to one life left and then they were going to run like hell.

"Nothing personal, Mr. Rich, but when you're down to the last one, we don't want to be anywhere near you."

"*Ha*ha." Laugh it up, guys. Who's keeping count?

SNIPERS MAKE YOU DO CRAZY SHIT!

COP Honaker-Miracle was a remote base, in Pech River Valley, Kunar Province, in Northeast Afghanistan by the Pakistan border, to which I had many missions. After getting settled in my room on one such mission and returning back to the Tactical Operations Center (TOC), a sergeant offered to take me out to the construction site. It was the middle of the night so I asked him if we could just do it in the morning. He said it was safer to visit the site at night because of sniper fire during the day.

"With our technology," he proudly pointed out, "we rule the night here."

Honaker-Miracle was one of the bases that was under continuous Taliban Sniper fire. It was in the same area of Afghanistan where a ferocious fire fight occurred that inspired the movie *Lone Survivor*. The film chronicled a covert Navy Seal operation in which 19 American soldiers lost their lives. Only one Seal made it out alive, and only due to the kindness of a group of Afghan villagers.

This was also in the vicinity where the *Restrepo* documentary was filmed. That film chronicled the perils faced by many American soldiers who risked their lives trying to clear the Korengal Valley of insurgents and gain the trust of the local population. It was considered one of the most dangerous areas in Afghanistan by the U.S. Military. Nearly 50 American soldiers died fighting there.

Some of my most memorable moments in Afghanistan occurred at Honaker-Miracle. It was the first base I traveled to at night by helicopter. Both Chinook and Blackhawk helicopters generally went out to the base once a week on a constantly changing schedule so the Taliban would not learn their routine.

I was helping construct masonry buildings on the base for the protection of U.S. soldiers. There was a memorial with several small monuments and permanent plaques around the flag pole honoring the combatants featured in both films, as well as other soldiers that had been killed in the area. The names of many brave soldiers are engraved on those plaques.

On my way to lunch one day, Taliban snipers started shooting at the dining hall building. Bullets were hitting the walls and metal fixtures. Hearing the pinging of bullets hitting the structure around me scared the hell out of me, so I dove for cover.

Squatting down behind a small concrete wall and trying to decide if I wanted to risk getting shot running to the dining hall for something to eat seemed crazy. I decided to stay put and eat some of the food bars I had in my backpack. As I was chewing a granola bar, an army captain came around the corner and asked me what I was doing.

After explaining I didn't want to get shot in the ass trying to get something to eat, he nodded his head and chuckled. He asked me if I had an extra snack I could spare. So we both sat there eating granola bars until the base sent a patrol out after the sniper. This is some crazy shit, I thought to myself.

The next day, I ran into sniper fire again as I walked between a couple other buildings and again dove for cover, this time next to a few soldiers. I felt kind of stupid asking them how I could get to the other side of the 20-yard opening, already knowing the obvious answer.

"All you have to do to get across this 'kill zone' is duck down and run like hell," they shouted to me.

"You're shitting me, right?" was the only reply that came to mind.

Since I had to get to the other side to work, I just had to suck it up, especially when I realized two of the others were preparing to run as well. I quickly agreed with the other guys that we would take turns running. When it came my turn I just said to myself, "1-2-3, run."

As I ran across the kill zone, I could hear the bullets hitting the buildings and gravel around me, but I had no idea how close they came to hitting me. Once on the other side, I was out of breath and my heart was racing like crazy. All of a sudden, I knew what having an 'adrenaline high' was all about. If I wasn't so damned scared, I would have thought it was pretty cool. Once my nerves settled down, I felt a little foolish realizing these soldiers did this for a living.

Later that day I was walking with two sergeants to another building on base under construction I needed to check. A sniper opened fire on us from outside the base. As we ran I could hear the ZIP-ZIP of the bullets hitting the gravel. The shots finally hit a water station with pallets full of bottled water. I saw a few hundred water bottles explode. I ducked behind a concrete wall for protection and just squatted there.

"Hey Mr. Walton, you're on the wrong side of the wall," I heard one of the sergeants yelling. I quickly crawled around to the other side where they were crouched down, laughing at my naiveté.

"How can you guys be laughing in a shit storm of bullets?" I thought.

Once on the right side of the wall with them, I picked up some gravel rocks and threw them over the top of the wall. They asked me what I was doing. I told them, "I've heard the only way you can earn a medal is if you return fire. So, I am returning fire."

One of them laughed and said, "You are one freaking crazy old man, Mr. Walton."

I guess being in a war zone makes you act crazy and do stupid shit sometimes.

I was still encountering more close calls than I had expected as a civilian contractor. Being subjected to enemy sniper fire inside the walls of a military base seemed a little strange.

Some bases hired Afghans to man the guard towers and protect us from Taliban attacks. At one base, we came under attack by Taliban. Nothing new. But what was new to me was that the Afghan guards in the tower abandoned ship and ran for cover. Our U.S. soldiers then had to rush to the towers and fight off the Taliban in their place.

When the fleeing Afghan guards were later asked why they didn't shoot back at the Taliban, their only defense was, "We thought we were hired to man the guard towers, not to shoot our cousins."

It looked like what we had there was not unlike the case of having the proverbial fox guarding the hen-house. I once again remembered the words of my old Lebanese bodyguards: "Welcome to Afghanistan, Mr. Rich."

WELCOME TO COP MONTI, CAPTAIN

On another mission to COP Monti, I was accompanied by a U.S. Army Captain, newly deployed to Afghanistan. As I was giving him a tour of the base and the usual orientation, I pointed out the directions from which incoming rocket attacks came and also where sniper fire was most likely to come from.

All of a sudden there were bullets zipping past our heads. We ran for cover immediately. The captain told me this was the first time he had been under fire or in combat and was proud he hadn't pissed in his pants. I told him I didn't know if this counted as being under fire in combat or not.

After things went silent, we worked our way around the walls only to find out that it was the ASG (Afghan Security Guard) and British trainer using their sniper rifles for outgoing target practice. I laughed and told the two they really had us going with the bullets going over our heads. I don't think the captain saw the humor in it. I guess it takes a few months to develop the sick sense of humor that seems to run rampant over there. The Afghan and the Brit laughed and said they didn't see us below them. Nothing like a little friendly fire to get your heart rate going.

A GRENADE WITH MY NAME ON IT?

As I was preparing to take a C-130 flight to FOB Sharana in the Paktika Province, in the Eastern side of Afghanistan near the Pakistan border, I was standing in line at the baggage scanner machine when an Army captains' vest came through the scanner. The visual screen showed the vest had a grenade on it. Being told grenades were not allowed on this flight, the Army officer took the Grenade off the vest and accidentally dropped it on the floor. As I watched the grenade bounce on the floor in front of me, everyone else around me ducked for cover - I stood there speechless. I simply watched, frozen in disbelief, waiting for the pin to pop out and the grenade to explode. I remember thinking to myself, "Oh shit, is this how I am going to die after all the enemy rockets and sniper bullets I've been able to dodge?"

Luckily, nothing happened. An airport employee who was obviously shaken and scared to death picked up the grenade and handed it back to the captain. She in turn handed it to a soldier staying behind on base.

ROCKETS OVER KANDAHAR – NO CASUALTIES, JUST PIZZA

While I was working at Kandahar, the base got its share of Taliban rockets hitting the area. Every time the sirens went off signaling an incoming barrage, we had to report to a concrete bunker. I did not hear of any fatalities occurring at Kandahar while I was there. In comparison to the remote bases I traveled to, I thought it to be a safer environment.

Still, it was a royal pain in the ass whenever we heard, "Incoming, Incoming!" It was a bitch having to run to the bunker at all hours of the day and night and sit there for a few hours at a time. There were no chairs or benches, only gravel on the ground. We couldn't stand up all the way because the bunkers had only about 5 feet head clearance inside.

In spite of being fatality-free, we did have one close call when a Taliban rocket landed in the middle of a Pizza Hut stand early in the morning. The explosion completely destroyed the Pizza Hut so I guessed we'd be going without pizza for a while. Luckily, no one was inside because of the early hour. If that rocket would have hit the place later in the day, it would have had a devastatingly different story to tell. We all laughed that the Taliban must not like pizza.

AFGHAN SOLDIERS: SOMETIMES THEIR OWN WORST ENEMIES

During one of my trips to FOB Fiaz, in the East near the Pakistan border, the base came under attack. FOB Fiaz didn't really have any hardened buildings so the fall back area was the Tactical Operations Center (TOC). As I was sitting in the TOC, I could see on the surveillance camera images of soldiers running around the base taking their positions. They had their vests and helmets on but were still wearing their P.E. shorts. They must have been working out and had no time to change into their regular uniforms.

After the attack subsided, I started hearing gun shots again. But this time it seemed like the Afghan National Army (ANA) and the Afghan National Police (ANP) were now shooting at each other from their perspective compounds just outside our base. I asked the soldiers in the TOC if that was possible and they told me, anything was possible at Fiaz.

"Only in Afghanistan can shit like this go down," one commented.

I just sat by until the shooting was over and then went back to work inspecting buildings. Just another typical day at the office.

GREEN ON BLUE ATTACKS: WHO'S THE REAL ENEMY?

Being on an Afghan base, whether an ANA (Afghanistan National Army), ABP (Afghan Border Patrol) or other type, was always a little un-nerving because of the "green-on-blue" attacks. These color-named assaults involved Afghan soldiers or Afghan policemen shooting American soldiers, or in my case American civilian contractors. Green referred to the Afghan Police and Afghan Army, Blue was the US/ NATO soldier or American contractor.

I found it quite naïve when some people back home would tell me I was not in danger on the bases because I was not a soldier carrying a weapon. I would quickly enlighten them, explaining the people doing the shooting don't care if you are a soldier or civilian, only that you're an American. You're just as dead either way.

NOT SURE I REACHED NINE, BUT I CAME CLOSE

Once I had accepted the fact that I could possibly die in Afghanistan, it took the pressure and worry off and I could get on with my work. Some of my martial arts training when I was a young adult had prepared me for this as I needed to be mentally strong to survive Afghanistan's furnace-like sun, arid desert, snow, high altitude, and other elements of this harsh environment.

At times I felt like a Shaolin monk traveling the countryside with no weapon. My frequently upset stomach and intermittent bouts with diarrhea made for many miserable days. Two of our sons are in the military, and one of them told me once, "To go where you go and do what you do with no military training and no weapon is nothing short of amazing."

Hearing the admiration in his voice really helped me keep going. I told him that I would have flashes in my mind where I was like the guy in the *Matrix* movie who would be transfixed into slow motion and bend like a contortionist when bullets were zipping toward him.

People were always asking me if I was worried about being killed. At first I had been petrified about this, but after surviving my first near death experience and then seeing others get killed around me while I survived, I placed my fate in God's hands and just kept moving forward.

Why did that last rocket land on top of someone else and not me? That was fate, or perhaps luck, or whatever you want to call it. I knew in many ways I had no control over whether or not I would get killed. It was up to God and I was OK with that.

I got to the point where I would laugh when I told people how sorry I felt for the guardian angel in heaven that got assigned to me. That guardian angel certainly had his work cut out for him.

TERRIBLE CONSEQUENCES

As dangerous as working conditions were for me, they were often more dangerous for the Afghans who worked on American-supervised construction projects. Even my interpreters would not let the people in their villages know who they worked for. They feared retribution from the Taliban who could be lurking anywhere, and yet every day they still showed up for work. They risked mutilation, torture and even death at the hands of the Taliban for themselves and their families.

One Afghan contractor who worked on a base where I was managing a construction project went to a nearby village to get supplies and materials. The Taliban found out he was working on an American base and cut off both his hands. How could he now support his family? How could I ever forget that? How could I ever stop hating the Taliban?

On another base, an American electrician who worked for me woke up one morning and took an early walk to the jobsite. As he walked around inspecting some work that had been done the previous day, he looked outside the perimeter wall and saw the severed head of one of the Afghan contractors who was working with us on the job. The head had been mounted on one of the tractors. We later learned that the Taliban had cut off his head as punishment and a warning to other Afghans not to work for the Americans.

I was horrified beyond belief. It was hard to fathom such incidents were actually happening on my job sites.

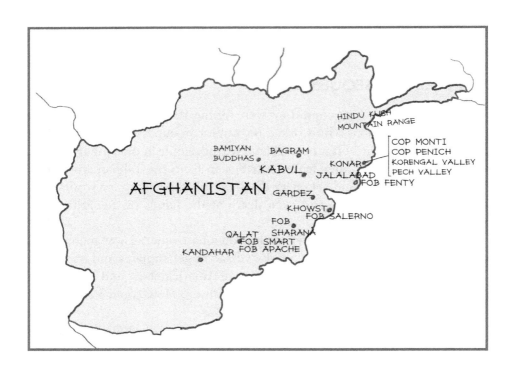

CHAPTER 12

"Afghan Good" Construction Methods

"You can use an eraser on the drafting table or a sledge hammer on the construction site."

—Frank Lloyd Wright

My lengthy background in architecture and building construction gave me a strong appreciation for the discipline of taking accurate measurements when planning and executing construction projects. While there is always a little leeway in certain situations, referred to as "tolerance," the art of just "winging it" does not fit when talking about construction methods...except for certain parts of Afghanistan.

It was not long after starting projects outside the wire (outside the bases) throughout Afghanistan that I realized the discipline of taking and adhering to accurate measurements was pretty much thrown out the window. Tape measures? What are those?

I knew I needed to be flexible as I had projects both inside and outside the bases. The Corp of Engineers projects that were inside the base required strict adherence to US Building Codes and measurements, but in remote areas off the bases, 'close' to the measurements and codes was good enough, hence the phrase "Afghan good."

The "Afghan good" concept was a novel idea. For most construction managers this would be a nightmare, but for me? I was looking forward to the challenge.

BUILDING CODES – ARE YOU KIDDING ME?

If you're building in remote Afghanistan, relax. There are no building codes.

While the first four sentences in this manual spell out the reality of the current situation, the rest of the manual lays out an entire set of rules and regulations to mandate most construction activities. I do see the need for some formal guidance in building practices. I am a realist, however, and I want to interject a few thoughts concerning the matter.

It appears we were expecting Afghan construction workers to make the huge jump from their methods and materials of construction to what America has evolved to over a 100+ year period. It just wasn't going to happen in a matter of a few years.

While some heroic efforts are being made on the educational front, the majority of Afghan people cannot yet read or write.

Here is an excerpt from USAID's initial document:

MANUAL OF BUILDING CONSTRUCTION FOR AFGHANISTAN
INTRODUCTION AND PURPOSE

Construction in Afghanistan is very different from U.S. construction and offers many challenges to maintaining good quality.

The availability of materials and equipment (or lack thereof) dictates most construction methods.

Outside of major cities, building designs seldom, if ever, have historically had any consideration for earthquake forces, but follow age-old methods without any modern building code influence.

There are currently no building codes in place, nor are there any controls placed by the government on contractor or engineer licensing or certification.

The Coalition Forces and international agencies have an opportunity with our current assistance effort to influence better building methods into the Afghan construction industry. The massive influx of dollars for infrastructure provides occasion to require Afghan contractors to adhere to near – if not entire – compliance with international building standards.

Most of the Afghans who worked on projects I supervised lived in mud brick houses with no electricity or running water. These folks were living in the shadows of Alexander the Great's castles built in 300 BC and we wanted them to understand and follow American building codes? As a person who lived and breathed the construction business in Afghanistan for four years in the current decade, all I can say is: It's gonna take time.

Alexander the Great's Castle After All These Centuries

A FOOT IS ONLY A FOOT

One of the problems the Afghan workers had was getting the spacing for nailing plywood sheathing on roofs, walls and floors in the correct measurement of 12 inches apart.

Out of desperation, I taught the Afghan workers to space the distance between framing nails by using their foot as a measuring device, give or take. I know that some feet are bigger than others, but it was close enough for the 12 inches called for in the drawings. Many of the workers could not read or write their own language, let alone understand drawings in English. I figured my foot measurement trick would fit right in with the "Afghan good" standard.

One day I was showing a contracting officer the work that had been done on one of my projects and the Afghan workers on the roof were yelling at me and pointing to their feet. The contracting officer asked me if they were insulting us. I laughed and explained they were simply expressing pride in their newly learned measurement skill and showing me they were applying what I taught them.

Now, I know what you're thinking – "Why didn't they just go out and buy a damn tape measure like we do at Home Depot?"

First, I must point out the concept of wood frame construction is totally foreign to the Afghans and many others in the Middle East. Almost all their structures are of the sun-dried brick variety construction. Outside the walls of many remote bases I visited were tents set up by nomads raising their sheep. This is how it was 3,000 years ago, and it's still the same today in many places.

Next, the availability of many things such as tape measures was next to none in these remote areas. You could only buy them in major cities hundreds of miles away. Plus, we had to deal with the fact that measurements on drawings might be in inches on some and meters on others. Teaching these Afghan workers the finer points of precise measurements was an exercise in futility. That wasn't going to work. Throw in the language barrier and things got even more interesting. In addition to most workers not being able to read or write in their own language, whether it be Dari or Pashto, the Pashtun language had different dialects in various parts of the country, creating difficulties for workers even speaking the same language.

I was working with locals who probably were sheep and goat herders before we hired them. When contractors supplied the new workers with boots, they often showed up the next day in their sandals again (we assumed they sold the boots). We were expecting these new folks to become semi-skilled in the framing, plumbing and electrical trades. That was wishful thinking at best. But since they really needed the work, they quickly learned to give the standard "no problem" reply when asked if they could do a specific task.

While having the rural Afghans master new skills was one thing, expecting them to become multi-talented in general construction was quite another. While I had no such expectations, I watched in amazement as they tried to do so. It was not unusual to see one of these unskilled workers trying like hell to function as a journeyman carpenter one day, and then transition to plumbing or electrical work the next.

The great thrill and reward for me was seeing their smiling faces on the job sites. They had jobs.

TEACHING CONSTRUCTION TECHNIQUES

Four thousand years ago, the concepts of math were basic at best, yet the Egyptians were able to achieve wonders without modern day equipment. I had to come up with creative ways to teach and apply construction techniques to Afghan workers using ancient building techniques, and the Afghans in turn showed me some of their methods.

I would show the workers an easy way to square up a building. Simply take a long piece of string and measure the two diagonals of the building. If the diagonals are the same length, the building is square. This was more than Afghan Good, it was Afghan Great!

Another useful "squaring up" method I taught them was an adaptation of the "3-4-5" rule often used by builders nowadays. This is a simple way to ensure a corner is a perfect 90-degree angle. It can be applied to corners of foundations, rooms, roofs, walls, etc. From the corner, measure three units along one wall, then four units the other direction. When the two endpoints are connected like a triangle, that third line should equal five units. When these measurements equal three, four and five, the corner is 90-degrees. Voila!

Based on the method the Romans used to build the aqueducts, the Afghans had a simple water level tool that didn't look like a tool at all, but just a very long piece of clear plastic tubing which they filled with water. A cool thing about this water level tool is that it can be used around corners and out of the "line of site," which a laser or builder's level cannot do. No wonder so many of ancient buildings are still standing. We can get a modern-day version of this water level tool at most building supply stores.

Using Afghan Water Level

I always carried a hand eye level with me for checking slope grades. The Afghan workers were always amazed how it worked. When we were measuring the grade of slopes, the Afghans would use their water level tube and I would use my hand-eye level and we would compare the results. They always came out the same. We had great laughs measuring the grades with each of our tools and coming up with the same results.

The lack of proper tools made it difficult to finish the jobs on time and meeting project deadlines was all but impossible. In spite of the schedule delays, I got a real kick out of working with these local workers, especially the ones in the remote villages who were mostly farmers and sheep-herders before and were now construction workers trying to support their families. It was fulfilling for me personally to share my construction knowledge with these eager-to-learn workers. I loved seeing the sparkle in their eyes as we worked together on construction techniques.

THE BRICK LAYER ALWAYS WINS?

One day I was talking with an Afghan brick layer on FOB Smart, instructing him on the proper way to construct a brick wall. I was explaining why it was important to get mortar on four sides of each brick to hold them together – not only top and bottom, but left and right sides as well.

Even though this is not the way he had been doing it in the past, I walked away believing he'd do it my way from that point on. When I returned the next day, he was back to doing it the Afghan way of just laying down a layer of mortar and stacking the bricks on top without also putting mortar between the sides of the bricks.

I talked with him about the technique for a while and realized the error of my ways. The Afghan method of not putting mortar between the bricks as they were placed side-by-side was the same method used in the construction of Alexander the Great's castles like the one on the hill above us. Since that was still standing after 2000 years, why change now?

Instead of arguing with his reasoning, I just laughed along with him and his friends. I remembered the saying about "having the wisdom to accept the things we cannot change," and decided I needed to develop a more compelling argument for proper brick laying.

SCRAPPY, THE WANNABE INTERPRETER

A constant problem out at the small remote sites was communicating with the Afghan workers. I had tried learning Pashto and Dari from my friends at Kabul House, and I took on-line courses and attended classes at both FOB Salerno and FOB Fenty, but I didn't learn enough to communicate as effectively as I wanted. So, I needed assistance from Afghan Interpreters.

I found an interpreter wannabe about 12 years old, named "Scrappy." He was an Afghan boy who worked on COP Penich in the Kunar Province doing odd jobs, picking up garbage, cleaning DFACs, whatever was needed. He made about $100 a month supporting his whole family of seven.

Scrappy and His Gang

Scrappy learned English from the US Soldiers at the outpost. I understand he also earned a trip to America for a few weeks, under some sort of foreign aid project to learn English. After he and his gang met me at the remote base, they began to follow me whenever I was there because they were curious about the work I was doing. They also seemed intrigued with my helmet and armor and wanted to try them on. I referred to Scrappy's buddies as his "gang" because they liked to mimic the mannerisms of gang members like those in the States.

On one occasion there were several U.S. Army Officers in the operations center at Penich, needing an interpreter to communicate with some Afghans. They couldn't find an Afghan interpreter at the time for some reason, so I asked them if it was sensitive or secret information. They said it was not, so I said I could get an interpreter for them in just a couple minutes.

I opened the door and yelled out to the Afghans standing outside to get me Scrappy. In a few minutes, Scrappy showed up and said to me in his best American gang voice while flashing gang signs with his hands, "Hey man, what do ya need man?"

The officers looked at the both of us like we had just arrived from a different planet. I laughed and introduced them to young Scrappy. They could not believe this young boy was going to translate the whole conversation for them.

Scrappy & Me

Scrappy wanted me to take him with me to be my personal interpreter wherever I went, even to go back to my base to live with me. I wish I could have, he was a great kid. Every time I traveled to COP Penich, I took Scrappy and his gang several boxes of candy. I even had my wife send me a few American T-shirts for Scrappy. He loved the fighting Duck shirt from the University of Oregon, my alma mater.

THE REBAR RULER

One day I helped an Afghan worker lay out the steel rebar on a foundation for a latrine building (bathroom) on a remote base and told him it would be exactly the same on the other building about 20 feet away.

Since these particular workers could not read or write, I showed them how to use a rock I had chosen (of the proper size) as a measuring tool for the spacing between the rebar and the concrete forms. For proper vertical alignment, I taught them to use a water bottle on a string as a plumb bob to make sure the columns were straight up and down.

When I came back to the site I would ask to see their measuring rock to make sure they were using the same one I gave them. On my first visit to see their progress, they smiled proudly as they produced the rock I taught them to use. When I looked at the work they had done thus far on setting the rebar for the foundation on the second latrine building, with the rock as their ruler, the rebar spacing was good between the rebar and the concrete forms for the foundation. But I just had to shake my head in disbelief seeing that the rebar coming up out of the foundation for the location of the walls and columns were not the same as the other building.

I asked Scrappy, my young local quasi-interpreter on this job, why aren't the rebar for the walls and columns in the same location as the other building? The local Foreman told Scrappy, "Sorry Mr. Rich, our brains don't always work."

I was so shocked by his response. How do you even respond to something like that? I just laughed, I didn't know what to say. Chalk that up to "Afghan Good."

The Afghan workers had a tough time comprehending the need for rebar in the first place. They don't use rebar in their village construction yet look around at all the ancient castles built thousands of years ago, still standing.

Since the concrete had already been poured, I knew tearing it up and re-doing the rebar was out of the question. I had to get creative with some retrofitting and additional bracing. Since it was only a one-story structure, it was an easy fix.

One of the most essential construction techniques I used was the one I developed myself for the Afghan workers. I called it the "Mr. Rich Measuring System." I explained to them that the distance between their thumb and little finger is about 6 inches and finger to elbow (forearm) is about 18 inches to make up for not having a tape measure. In keeping with the body part measuring system, I taught them mortar joints between bricks should be the thickness of their pointing finger. Afghan good!

In all honesty, I cannot take all the credit for coming up with the brilliant idea of using a human male foot to approximate 12 inches, or a finger thickness to indicate the size of mortar spacing, and such. I remembered from some of my studies in architecture classes in college how the ancients used the human body as a measuring tool, so I tried to implement some of these in teaching the Afghan workers.

HOW DEEP IS THE WELL? JUST COUNT!

The Afghan soldiers on one of their bases showed me a water well pipe they wanted to use for drinking water that didn't work. The pump was gone. To get materials to get this working, we needed to know how far down to the water level. They did not have any measuring tapes, string or anything to put down the well to find out how far it was down to the water level, so I showed an Afghan Colonel a technique of dropping a small rock down the pipe into the well and count 1001, 1002 and so on until we heard it hit the water and splash. I explained to him that an object falls at about 16 feet per second, so we multiplied 16 times the four seconds it took to hear the splash to be about 60 feet to the surface of the water. Back at FOB Apache I suggested installing a hand pump, as the Afghans would not be able to sustain a generator, its fuel and maintenance to keep an electric pump working.

A NEW TOP-DOWN APPROACH

"What goes around comes around."

On one of my trips to a remote base, COP Monti, as a favor I brought with me some cartons of milk for a British associate remembering he had complained of not having milk and the Brits simply cannot drink their tea without milk. I asked nothing in return. Since the favor had real meaning, one day, the Brit called me to my surprise and said an Afghan contractor working on one of my projects was making concrete for some structural columns without adding rock to the mixture. It was a crucial 'heads-up' alert.

I flew out to the site right away to check the columns. Sure enough, I could tear off a piece of the column with my bare hand. One cannot do this with solid concrete. My British buddy lived on the base where the project was underway so he had been keeping an eye on it in my absence. He knew I could only get there once every week or so to inspect things. I had not even asked him to do this, but his returning my favor saved a great deal of time and materials.

I told the contractor the columns had to come down and went to inspect some of the other buildings being constructed at the base. I couldn't believe what I saw when I returned. There was an Afghan worker on top of the column, 20 feet up in the air, with several rebar sticking straight up out of the top of the column pointing at the Afghan's ass. He was bent over using a sledge hammer knocking the cement from underneath his feet. I guess he figured he would work his way down the column to the ground. He was lucky he didn't get impaled by the rebar. That was just plain nuts and crazy. It was one of those situations where the visual image wants to make you cringe and yet roar with laughter at the same time. The Afghan top down approach!

I told the contractor to get his worker the hell off of there before he killed himself. The contractor did make the worker get down off the column and use a safer approach. I was pretty sure the worker went right back up on the top of that column after I left the base. The Afghan workers often think our requirements are stupid. After all, who are these Americans to tell them how to do the work?

ONLY IN AFGHANISTAN!
YIKES! BAD IDEA – He was knocking the concrete out from under himself.

REBAR JUMPER CABLES

I witnessed many events that were both humorous and sad. This one makes you laugh when you know you really shouldn't be laughing.

I drove an SUV out to a job site right around daybreak and forgot to turn the lights off. When I tried starting the vehicle up several hours later, the battery was dead. There was another vehicle nearby so I asked the workmen to see if they could find some jumper cables as I also went off to look for a set in our conex office on site. When I came back to the SUV, I saw one of the workers about to fire up the SUV while another was holding his idea of makeshift jumper cables. I could see these 'jumper cables' were actually two pieces of steel rebar the guy had bent to suit the purpose, I yelled for them to stop. Too late. When the one worker turned the ignition switch, there was a huge spark and the other guy holding the rebar was knocked on his ass a few feet away from the SUV. Only in Afghanistan.

As the elated worker picked himself up, dusted himself off and gave me a wide grin and a thumbs up, I had to force myself to stop laughing. Their ability to cleverly improvise to solve a problem impressed the creativity in me. On the other hand, their naiveté was a somewhat sad reality that constantly endeared them to me.

ANOTHER FINE MIXER YOU GOT US INTO

On another job site, I was walking by a small concrete mixer and I kept hearing a banging sound but could not see anyone hammering. I was about to look inside the mixer when a worker stuck his head out from inside. It scared the shit out of me. Here was this guy, inside the mixer out in the burning hot sun, chiseling out all the dried concrete.

I couldn't figure out how he had gotten in there. I had often suggested to the Afghan contractors they should clean the cement from the mixers at the end of each day with water, both inside and out. I don't think it dawned on them that washing the wet concrete away would keep it from hardening in the mixer, which made it very tough to operate.

Man in Small Portable Concrete Mixer - His way of cleaning it!

I'm sure they thought this was just another stupid American requirement we made up to create extra work for them. So rather than wash out the mixer at the end of the day, their solution for cleaning it was to crawl inside and chip away the concrete AFTER it hardened. As I stood there dumbfounded, scratching my head in disbelief, one of the workers came up to me and asked, "What is the problem, Mr. Rich?

FLASH TO ASH

One project on a remote base, a one-story plywood B-Hut, to be used for sleeping quarters, was required by US specs to be finished with oil-based paint inside and out. The local Afghan contractor building this did not understand what oil-based paint was. His solution was to mix diesel fuel in with the water-based latex paint to make, in his mind, oil-based paint. After being notified that the building was done, I went to check it out and saw the latex cans laying on the ground. "Oh shoot, you were supposed to use oil-based paint."

His reply: "No Problem, Mr. Rich. We mixed diesel into the paint to make it oil-based paint!"

In shock, my hands went to my head, "OMG ... What you have created by using this diesel-based paint is a building that is Flash-to-Ash in 10 Seconds!" Only in Afghanistan. I love working in this place. The building got repainted with correct paint.

I SAY DRAWING, YOU SAY MAP

On a number of my projects, I saw an obvious disconnect between the expectations of my American bosses and the realities of the Afghan workers. I did lots of projects at one particular Afghan Security Guard (ASG) compound, a base I liked to call "Happy Camp" because the workers and guards were always happy to see me.

I always made it a point to walk up to every worker and say hello to them and thank them for doing a good job. They were not used to such treatment by other Americans, who were often yelling at the Afghan workers and treating them like a bunch of idiots. Uneducated, I would agree with, but many of these hardworking guys were anything but idiots. I saw this as one of the pleasant challenges for "winning the hearts and minds" of the Afghan people.

To this end, I always made sure the workers felt they were respected members of the team by chatting with them as best I could over tea about the details of the project. I was able to establish a great rapport with the workers in spite of the language barrier. I sought their input with the help of my interpreter and incorporated it whenever I could. Naturally, I had to exercise caution and do it sparingly to avoid jeopardizing the project, but simply allowing them to have input was all that was required. When I instituted procedures contrary to their stated desires, they accepted them in earnest since they knew I had at least listened to their side before making a decision.

One hard and fast rule my American bosses followed like an edict was that there always had to be a complete set of engineering drawings on every job site.

"Without drawings, there is no order," was the mantra they lived by.

During my first visit to this particular jobsite, I asked the workers if they had a set of drawings. Scrappy, who was my interpreter sidekick again on this job, explained to me the workers refer to drawings as maps, because they look like road maps to them. So, we asked if they had a "set of maps."

The leader of the worker crew quickly got a couple 8 ½ x11 drawings/ maps and proudly showed them to me. The drawings were so faded and stained you couldn't read them, but they felt confident they were in complete compliance with the rules as they had their maps at the site. I kept up the façade for their sake and forged ahead with construction. Sometimes you just have to make allowances, especially when the workers were risking their lives from the Taliban for working on these projects.

Drawings OK, Mr. Rich?

PICKING ROCKS

A load of gravel was delivered to a site I was inspecting where we were building a huge concrete slab. The gravel was the wrong size, way too many big rocks in it. I asked the contractor to have the right size gravel delivered. Instead, his solution was to bring in a couple laborers to pick out the big rocks. That was one of the craziest ideas I have ever heard. It took several weeks for them to do this. Every day I drove by the site and would watch these guys pick out the big rocks, put them in a wheelbarrow and wheel it to a new pile. It seemed to me it would have been easier just to bring in the right size material, but Afghan labor in many cases was cheaper than materials.

SUB-CONTRACTING MUSICAL CHAIRS

I found there to be a huge disconnect between the Afghan contractors awarded the building projects and the actual workers on the related job sites. Sometimes the project had been subcontracted several times. Each time the job was sub-contracted out, that left less money to actually build the project. Quite often the original Afghan contractor didn't have any idea of what was going on at the job site and the workers on the job site didn't even know who they actually worked for. I knew of one building that should have been done a year before with the Afghans still working on it and a medical aid building that should have been started a year before which the contractor had never started. Here we were a year later, and we had to get this construction going.

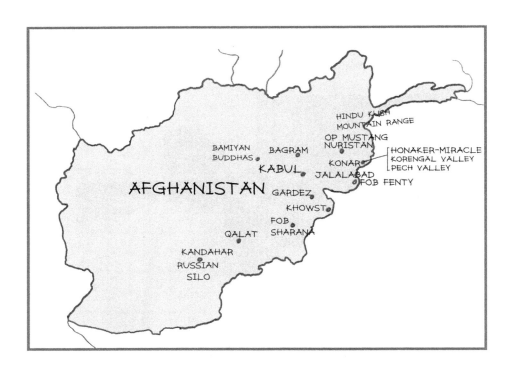

CHAPTER 13

The Lighter Side

"Happiness is the meaning and the purpose of life, the whole aim and end of human existence."

—Aristotle

In Afghanistan, I worked with a whole bunch of guys that were 50+ years old. As a combined group, the others on the base referred to us as the "gray beards." We had more than just grayness in common. Virtually every one of us had come to work in Afghanistan for one reason: we needed the job.

THE GRAY BEARDS

Our gray beard community was chock full of people in various trades, including plumbers, electricians, carpenters, mechanics, engineers, architects, planners, and so on. The diverse backgrounds we brought to the table fueled a steady stream of entertaining life stories.

There were a few in the group who had not lost their income due to the recession, but had been drawn into the overseas contracting world only because the jobs paid significantly more than comparable ones in America. There was the building inspector from North Carolina who smoked three packs of cigarettes a day, the former owner of a concrete business in Utah who had a fiery temper, and the colorful Texan, an overweight electrician who had been working contracts all around the world most of his life. This guy was in his 50's and never married. I used to kid him about his habit of buying jewelry for the laundry girls just to earn their smiles. The list went on and on.

ROLLOVER TRAINING

While we civilian contractors did not have to go through basic training like soldiers do, we did have to complete several online training courses and a bunch of training exercises before we went overseas and even more when we get there, and then on a yearly basis. Who would've thought you needed continuing education to work in a war zone.

We were not allowed to travel with military convoys out to job site locations without first completing a training exercise called rollover training.

The exercise prepares people how to react and protect themselves if the vehicle they're in rolls over. The military had rollover simulators set up on bases. Basically you're seat-belted into a Humvee or MRAP while it does barrel rolls like a cement mixer.

After arriving in Afghanistan, I was asked to go off base to look at some construction sites for the RCC (Regional Contracting Command). First I needed to complete rollover training to be able to convoy outside the wire, but civilians were not allowed to take the rollover training. How's that for a typical military catch-22?

I told the Regional Contracting Command that I was not allowed to take the rollover training and voila! We received a letter from a U.S. Marine Officer at Bagram, and they changed the policy so I could go out to look at their jobsites.

Now that it was once again open to civilians, we had a few crazy factors come into play during rollover training. One civilian I met really wanted the training and signed up for it. He was obviously in no physical shape to even think about going outside the wire for any reason. And not going outside the wire by definition meant he would never be riding in a military convoy.

After explaining there was no need for him to be trained for rollovers since he would not be leaving the base, I also pointed out that he could be hurt because there is some danger involved – especially for someone not in great physical shape. He of course didn't listen to me and took the training anyway. While flipping upside down in the rollover simulator, he got choked out by the safety straps and had to be taken to the hospital.

Believe me, as is the case with many training exercises, the rollover simulator can produce some good chuckles if you watch long enough. One gal got in the Humvee and put her safety straps on backwards. In order to get her out of the contraption, a guy had to manipulate her to release the buckles.

"I'll have to feel around to unbuckle the straps, so please don't think I'm trying to molest you," he said to her in his most serious voice.

"No problem, just get me the hell out of here," she muttered in frustrated embarrassment.

There was one lady who was hanging upside down when she released her straps and didn't remember to put her hands above her head to protect her fall. Naturally, she went straight down headfirst into the gun turret on the roof and almost knocked herself out. I just could not stop laughing.

A MICROWAVE FOR CHRISTMAS

The U.S. Soldiers at OP Mustang didn't have much of anything except a great view. Their old plywood buildings were as sparse as I had seen. The Air Force

Master Sergeant in charge sent me out to Mustang to draw plans for a few new buildings to brighten up the surroundings for the soldiers stuck at this lonely post.

Observation Point Mustang

It was near Christmas on this particular visit to Mustang. The trip included an Air Force electrician sent to do a bunch of wiring for the generator that supplied electricity for the post. The soldiers pointed out the claymore mines they had put on the fence positioned for enemy attacks so the electrician and I would not accidentally bump them. I always got a kick out of the wording on the mines: "Point this side toward the ENEMY".

I enjoyed bringing the guys cigarettes, chewing tobacco and treats the Air Force troops at my base had me deliver to them. While we were having lunch, the soldiers pulled out a few packages of microwave popcorn they just received in care packages from home.

"Do they really think we have a microwave out here in the middle of nowhere?"

When I returned to base, I went to the USO with my Master Sergeant and talked to the supervisor, a cute lady from Georgia. With her sweet Southern drawl and her cargo shorts, we were sure she had the officers in charge wrapped around her little finger. We told her about my soldier friends stuck up there at Mustang all alone with their popcorn and no microwave for making it.

"Darlene, do you think you might be able to talk your bosses into donating a microwave for those lonely troops up there?"

A little later she showed up at our office followed by an Army officer carrying a microwave. With a little wink, she said, "Tell those brave boys up there Merry Christmas from Darlene and the USO."

It was Christmas Eve when I caught the next helicopter flight headed for OP Mustang, microwave in hand. Accompanying me on the flight were a female news correspondent and a cameraman from CBS. They were filming "On Top of the World," a Christmas special, to air on television back home. As I got off the helicopter carrying the microwave, the soldiers came out to meet us. "Merry Christmas from Darlene and all the guys at the USO," I smiled. As they reached out to grab the microwave, I said, "You guys didn't have to walk all the way down here to the landing zone to meet me."

"Sure we did," they said. "At your age, we were afraid you'd drop the damn thing carrying it up the hill." The soldiers and the CBS crew had a big laugh at my expense.

As soon as we got inside the plywood building, the guys plugged it in and we all sat around eating microwave popcorn. This military unit was from Hawaii so we had a lot of fun talking about the Hawaiian Islands and surfing. I have surfed in Hawaii, California and Oregon, so we had lots of stories to share.

The correspondent listened as we talked about surfing, so entertained with our hand gestures like we were riding our boards together. Suddenly she exclaimed; "Here you guys are, thousands of miles from the ocean, up here at 7,000 feet elevation 'on top of the world' talking about surfing. I never expected to see this in Afghanistan."

Later that day I was invited for Chai tea with the local elders and interpreters. We met in a small stone building that had AK-47 rifles hanging all over the walls. The correspondent from CBS was not allowed to join us because she was female. Too bad because that would have added a nice little touch to the TV special.

My wife later told me she saw the CBS special on TV and thought it was pretty cool. She was even able to see me carrying the microwave off the helicopter.

CHRISTMAS REUNION WITH MY NEPHEW

One Christmas, I learned my Nephew in the Army was deployed to another base in Afghanistan called "Russian Silo." Finding out he was coming to KAF to have his MRAT trucks worked on, I treated him and his squad to pizza, cases of energy drinks and lots of laughs. My nephew's soldiers had fun saying thank you "Uncle Rich". Here we are, a Christmas family reunion on the other side of the earth in war torn Afghanistan with guns and pizza. Months later after he was back home with his family, I traveled to Russian Silo for a job and learned the US Soldiers were getting one hot meal a day and eating MRE's (meals ready to eat) and individual cups of cereal the remainder.

FUN & GAMES

Soldiers come up with all kinds of things to keep themselves entertained, amused and not going nuts. On a return trip to Honaker, I brought with me a contracting officer, an Air Force Captain. The Lieutenant and Sergeant at Honaker asked the Captain and me if we played ping pong. "Sure," I said, "but it has been a long time."

The ping pong table was in a small room against a wall. They invited us to play a friendly game, then proceeded to tell us they play by different rules. Their game is called Scar Ball meaning when you score a point, the other team has to pull up their t-shirt, turn around and expose their backs so you can slam a ping-pong ball into their back leaving a welt, a red temporary scar. When the Captain and I scored our first point, I hit the ball into one of the guys' backs and they laughed saying, "is that all you got, old man?" After that I didn't hold back and neither did they. I did notice that I was getting the majority of the hits on my back, rather than my partner, the Captain. What the shit? They all laughed saying, "the Captain outranks us, plus we like to hear you yell when you get hit."

They also introduced the Captain and me to Cornhole. It's a game like Horse Shoes, tossing small sand bags through a hole in a propped up board. The Honaker difference is we played at night with a glow stick in the hole so you could see where to aim. Plus, they were monitoring and calling in air strikes in between games. We'd watch the air strikes on the monitors in the TOC, then go back to playing our game of Cornhole in the dark. Only in Afghanistan.

BABY IN THE BUCKET

At another base, we competed to see who saw the most people riding on a motorbike or scooter at one time during our visits to the cities or villages throughout Afghanistan. My highest number was five people on one scooter. But the winner saw seven people on one motorbike. By far my favorite was a baby that I saw in a five-gallon bucket. There was a man driving with a lady seated behind him on the motorbike, and the lady was holding a bucket with a baby in it in one hand. She held the bucket out from the motorbike as they drove down the street. That was one of the craziest and most dangerous things I have ever seen.

SOUTHWEST AIRLINE NUTS

A co-worker received some boxes of Southwest Airline peanut packages. On my next flight, I gave them to gate attendants to hand out to the soldiers as they went through the gate, flying to remote bases. They had fun. To get a package of nuts on a flight in a war zone was such a shock to everyone, bringing a little bit of home and laughter to a war zone. I'm sure Southwest Airlines had no clue their nuts were such a joy and a great morale builder to our troops.

HORSE SOLDIERS

While I was at a very remote base, the Special Forces horses broke out of their corral and got on the helicopter landing pad, reminding me of the book *Horse Soldiers*. It was a great show watching the soldiers run around trying to round up the horses so the helicopters could come in for a landing. I wish I had a video of that day. Some soldiers were on foot and some in their Gater ATV chasing the horses around to get them back into their corral. I remembered the frustration of trying to catch our own horses at home when they did not want to get caught. Sitting there watching reminded me how fortunate I was to be up front and close to the action rather than being back in the office on one of the big bases. I loved my job.

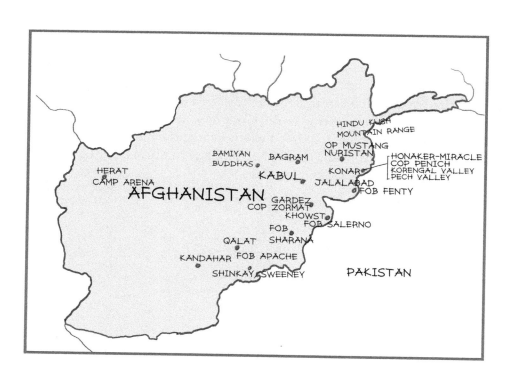

CHAPTER 14

Have Backpack, Will Travel

"Life is either a daring adventure or nothing."
—Helen Keller

Aside from the many months I stayed at Kabul House, I mostly traveled around Afghanistan by myself with a backpack and my sleeping bag. I imagined myself as a modern-day Lawrence of Arabia traveling across Afghanistan. It gave me the opportunity to live – and almost die – through some scary but great experiences. Because of my flexibility and eagerness to work on construction projects in the middle of nowhere, I got to see a lot of Afghanistan most people will never see.

Traveling around the country from base to base and project to project gave me a sense of real freedom. As long as I was working on projects for whichever organization was paying me at the time, I could control my own destiny. However that freedom of choice came with a price tag. In exchange for the freedom to go my own way. I had to give up much of the security protection I enjoyed during the early days living at Kabul House. I no longer had Lebanese PSD or Afghan bodyguards watching over me at every turn.

The freedom I had as a civilian contractor allowed me to be very productive in accomplishing tasks for all sorts of organizations. I was able to move around Afghanistan quite freely, assisting in designing and overseeing construction projects for both US and Afghan military, even doing some projects for the Navy Seals and other US Special Forces. Some of the bases and job sites were so close that walking was often the most expedient ways to get there.

A lot of the soldiers I met in my travels found it unbelievable that I was working in hostile territory week in and week out with no weapon. I knew of no other person in Afghanistan doing what I was doing, and I did not carry a weapon because I was not a soldier. I was like a hired gun but instead of a gun belt, I wore a tool belt and carried lots of drafting paper.

HITCH-HIKING IN A WAR ZONE?

Since I did not have my own armored vehicle but still had to get out to many remote bases and job sites on a regular basis, I realized I had a problem. Finding transportation to my various destinations took some creativity. There is no Travel Agent to help one move around the Afghan countryside. I guess I could have waited for my various "bosses" to arrange transportation for me, but that would have wasted valuable time.

I had to become an expert at hitching rides on all kinds of planes, helicopters and military convoys. When you see one of those war movies showing the troops jumping out the back of a Chinook helicopter or C-130 cargo plane wearing helmets and body armor, think of me. On many days, that's how I went to work.

My biggest fear with this type of air travel was falling down getting on and off or having my helmet blown off by the jet engines or helicopter prop wash because they don't turn the engines off. Once I almost ran into the 50-caliber machine gun on the tail gate of a Chinook as we were exiting the helicopter. That would have been embarrassing. Needless to say, there were no airport concourses or jet-ways where I was going.

When I was in a meeting with the base commander at Camp Arena in Herat Province, I found out there were stories about my travel exploits circulating around the various bases. When I first sat down with the colonel, he leaned toward me and said, "I've been wondering who the civilian with a beard is, walking around my battlespace wearing a multi-cam uniform." He grinned and continued, "I understand you've been whoring yourself out to all my military units to get rides out to your jobsites."

I laughed and replied, "Pretty much sir."

After that first meeting, I was called into his office on several occasions to give him quick briefings on what I was doing. He was a great American soldier not prone to beating around the bush. He reminded me of General Patton.

One ride I got was in a Stryker armored vehicle from FOB Sweeney to FOB Apache. Dust from the dirt roads infiltrated the vehicle for the entire 2-hour drive. By the time the Stryker reached FOB Apache, we were all covered in dust from head to toe. I caught a look at myself as we exited the Stryker. I was taking my sun glasses off when I saw that I had a severe case of raccoon eyes. I think I looked like one of General Rommel's men in the African desert during World War II.

Mr. Rich Hitching a Ride on a Stryker

HELICOPTER RIDES

I often rode in helicopters, flying way above the danger. Some of those were military choppers equipped with side or rear gunners. But not all the helicopters I was able to hop rides in were military. I also hitched rides on civilian choppers such as those from Molson Air, AAR Corp., or Presidential Airways. My sentimental favorites were the birds from Columbia Helicopter and Evergreen Helicopter because they were both headquartered in Oregon, where I was from.

Canada's Molson Air Huey's from Molson Beer Brewing Company, which were being rented for use in Afghanistan, must've also flown skiers up into the Canadian mountains, because their warning sign you walked past listing the rules to board the helicopter included a cartoon picture of a snowy mountain with a person getting his head cut off if he didn't duck for the helicopter blades.

I rode these Molson helicopters so much, the pilots would joke, "Hey, Mr. Rich, could you please give the preflight briefing today?" I instructed with hand gestures explaining the "GO Bag," the SAT phone, boarding and dismounting the helicopter, avoidance of the props and what to do during a crash landing, such as dragging the pilots out of the aircraft if they are injured.

WHERE IS SCRAPPY WHEN I NEED HIM?

One challenge I faced during my backpacking adventures was the language barrier. I had no interpreter with me like I had during the time I worked out of Kabul House. And since Scrappy, the wannabe interpreter, was only available around COP Penich in Kunar, I often had to fend for myself language-wise.

One trick I used to handle the problem was to carry a few signs with me with standard phrases written in the various languages. At Camp Arena where I spent lots of time, I had to deal with a linguistic crossfire of sorts on a daily basis. The base, which was on one side of the Herat airport, was run by the Italians with guards at the gates who did not speak English. On the opposite side of the airport was an Afghan air base I was helping to build, where everyone only spoke Dari.

I had to drive myself back and forth between the two bases in a small pickup truck cutting across the Herat International Airport runways. In addition to driving the air traffic controllers and airport security guys nuts, I had to deal with the language barriers at the security gates of both bases to gain entry. With the help of Afghan and Italian interpreters, I made 8 ½ x 11 paper signs in each language to show the guards. Another dilemma solved.

Please Let Me On Base

During my many months of scurrying about the Afghan countryside do-ing projects wherever I could find them, word was spreading about this crazy American construction guy helping to build all kinds of stuff. It wasn't long before the various commands and support organizations knew I was avail-able to work on almost any kind of construction-related job.

Even if they didn't find me, I often found them. I took on all kinds of proj-ect work: site designs, inspections, building renovations, shooting ranges, and architectural drawings for whatever was needed. I was the "have pen-cil will travel" go-to guy in Afghanistan. I carried a T-Square instead of an M-16. I may not have been able to kill the Taliban, but I could at least design protection against them.

SLEEPLESS IN AFGHANISTAN

One of the challenges of traveling to the remote bases was finding a place to sleep. Some of the FOBs and COPs had larger tents called 'transient' tents, which had metal bunk beds. There could be anywhere from 5 to 50 bunk beds arranged in dormitory style. Beds were available on a first-come, first-serve basis – just find a vacant bunk and claim it by piling your stuff on it.

The atmosphere inside these transient tents had all the ambiance of a high school football locker room. The soldiers had even created a name for the familiar odor. It smelled just like "feet and ass." There was not much heat and of course no air conditioning anywhere. Miserably hot in the summer and damn cold in the winter. Take it or leave it. Many times in the winter I would sleep with my clothes and stocking hat on inside my sleeping bag.

The lights inside these tents were off most of the time because there were guys sleeping during both the day and night hours depending on the shifts they worked. If you wanted to read or work on your laptop privately or in a more relaxed atmosphere, you had to hang blankets around a lower bunk so you wouldn't waken the soldiers.

Some of the remote bases would be hard pressed to find a bunk for me when I arrived. "We're not really set up for visitors staying overnight," was the phrase that spelled trouble. It usually meant I was shown to some small corner of a tent or wooden shack with little or no heat and a mattress on the floor that smelled like piss. At one base, I even slept on the floor in the mess hall.

Lying on a cot in the middle of the night, I would often hear camel spi-ders running across the floor. Using the flash-light I always kept nearby, I'd chase the spider across the tent in my underwear and use my boot to kill it. While the insects, spiders, scorpions and mice in these sleeping quarters made sleeping in peace difficult, it got worse. Those pests attract snakes and the poisonous variety are common in Afghanistan. Another way to be killed. I always had to turn my boots upside down in the morning to be sure there wasn't a scorpion inside.

SPAGHETTI & MEATBALLS ANYONE?

Availability of meals at these remote bases varied greatly depending on a number of factors. Some bases had a mess tent or shack that served three meals a day. Though not to be mistaken as fine dining, this represented the high end. Some of the smaller bases only had one hot meal a day and the only other food was the ever-present MRE (Meal Ready to Eat) in a package. Oh boy ... my favorite ... spaghetti and meatballs in a packet.

I would get upset when I was at the larger bases with full-blown cafeterias and heard people whining and bitching about the food. "Get over it," I would think to myself, "Why don't you come with me to one of the combat outposts and see what those guys have to eat?"

I always carried Clif and granola food bars with me in my backpack. Chocolate chip was my favorite. Due to my unpredictable arrival times at the bases, I frequently missed meal times and the Clif Bars were the only things standing between me and an empty stomach. Of course, there were the times I would eat with the local Afghan people at different job site locations and that was always interesting. I made sure I always carried a few bottles of Imodium in my backpack because diarrhea followed many meals.

NICE SEEING YOU AGAIN, HONAKER

I traveled to many different bases throughout Afghanistan; many looked the same, yet they were all different in their own way. As a civilian contractor, I was treated quite differently from base to base. At some, I was treated as an inconvenience or maybe just a pain in the ass. At others, I was greeted with open arms as a welcome visitor.

The folks at Honaker-Miracle treated me like a friend they were always glad to see. They were very appreciative that I would risk traveling out to their base at all because of the danger of being killed. They also knew it was difficult for me since flights were sometimes available only once a week.

There was a strong perception at these remote bases that the U.S. Engineers didn't want to leave the comforts of the big bases like Bagram and Kandahar to check on the remote base projects. Because of the danger and marginal living conditions, they also believed that after a first visit by an engineer or construction manager, chances were slim they'd ever see that person again. But the troops at Honaker knew that lack of availability of a helicopter flight was the only reason they wouldn't see me on a regular basis.

The infrequency of flights was a serious hurdle and no one knew that better than the troops at this base, and of course, me. The importance of each mission and the intensity of sniper fire and mortar attacks were the critical decision factors when it came time for scheduling flights. Sometimes they would fly and sometimes not. It was a crap shoot.

Flights might take place either during the day or in the darkness of night depending on the conditions at the base. It was not unusual to be stuck at Honaker for a week at a time due to the irregularity and sparsity of flights.

When I was at a remote base, I'd always have to be ready to fly at a moment's notice with everything in my backpack. Whenever the helicopter would show up, I had to run to get on board or risk being stuck at the base for another week.

I really got a kick out of the helicopter rides to and from Honaker. Sometimes we were flying so close to the mountains I felt like I could reach out and touch them. The mountain tops were snow-covered most of the time, making for some pretty beautiful scenery – like the Rockies. Other times we were flying at night weaving in and out between the mountain peaks. I never knew when the soldiers on board would start firing the machine guns at enemy positions along the route.

HOLY SHIT, THIS IS A COMBAT MISSION

One of the most memorable flights I had while in Afghanistan was one I caught from FOB Fenty to Honaker-Miracle. It was an awesome experience. At Fenty, I was taken to a part of the base I had not seen before. This was a different staging area for the Chinook helicopters, not the regular HLZ.

At the staging area were a whole bunch of American soldiers carrying their duffle bags and weapons, ready to go. It was around midnight when they had me get in line with the soldiers and march onto the helicopter. Everyone stacked their duffle bags in the middle of the chopper and sat back along the sides. The pile of bags was so high, I could not see the soldiers on the other side. The load master was crawling across the top of the bags, moving things around and making sure everything was secure.

The only light on inside the Chinook was red, casting a fuzzy red glow throughout the whole inside of the bird, creating a surreal atmosphere. It felt like I was on a combat mission in a movie. Then it hit me smack upside the head. This *was* a combat mission! And I sure as hell was not in a movie. This was as real as it gets.

We had a gunner on each side of the bird and one at the ramp in the rear, all pointing their large machine guns out toward the dark landscape. A flash of panic hit me when I realized that the chopper could actually get shot down and if that happened, we were all screwed. I didn't know where those brave soldiers were going but they definitely had their warrior faces on. Not a word was said after we took off. I just sat there in the quiet.

I could see out the side gunner's window and with the brightness of the moon, I watched snow-capped mountain tops zoom by as we weaved through them. This always reminded me of the *Lost Horizons* novel by James Hilton, describing Shangri-La in the Himalayas. The mountains in Afghanistan are beautiful. The chopper finally sat down and I had no idea where in the hell we were. The soldiers got off carrying their bags as I watched them march off into the darkness.

When I finally arrived at the base, the moon was so bright it was like a spot light was on me and I could see my shadow stretching out across the dirt. I walked off the chinook feeling the warm air from the chopper's engines blowing on me. In the moonlight, I spotted the soldier sent out to meet the flight.

All of the visual images – the sounds of the props, the smell of diesel fuel, the heat from the engines, and the dust and rocks being thrown around – engulfed me as a noisy backdrop to my thoughts of the soldiers being dropped off to face the ultimate danger.

BUSINESS TRAVEL IN A WAR ZONE

Going to construction job sites and business meetings was a monumental task in this undeveloped and often hostile environment. In America you grab your brief case, a pencil and paper and off you go. In Afghanistan, you grab your bullet proof vest, case of bottled water, and a super deluxe first aid kit with blood clot packets that cost around $500 in case you were shot.

Depending on when I was there, in my first job I needed to bring along my Lebanese bodyguards and several Afghan security specialists all toting AK-47s. Now, I traveled under the protection of U.S. or other military forces. Only with the proper preparation could we drive to a meeting or construction site, still not certain we would come back alive. While the business environment in America is more competitive, it pales in comparison when considering the degree of difficulty in a war zone.

Many times I got stuck out at remote bases such as COP Zormat, outside the city of Gardez in Paktia Province in Eastern Afghanistan near the Pakistan border, because of snow, fog, heavy rain, Taliban attacks, etc. When such incidents would occur, many regular helicopter flights were cancelled, and I had to go to the operations center to find out when the next flight was due in. That could be a matter of days, by the way.

Oftentimes, unscheduled helicopters would come in without much notice, so I checked for incoming flights several times around the clock. At times I would find myself sitting in the landing zone areas with my packed bags for up to four hours at a time just waiting and ready to go at a moment's notice. When and if the choppers came in, they didn't usually stay for long.

After learning all the flights had been cancelled one time heading back to my base, I sat waiting patiently at the Zormat HLZ when unexpectedly, in his own helicopter, a U.S. Army colonel flew in for a meeting. I introduced myself to him and during our conversation, learned that he was going back to FOB Salerno, where I was stationed at that time, I asked if I could get a ride back with him. 90 minutes later, we were in the air headed to Salerno.

It was then I realized that networking and getting to know as many people as I could would be an important factor in me getting around efficiently in Afghanistan.

I knew that in order to be effective, I would often have to take the initiative to get things done on my own. What happened on one mission might not happen on the next. Thinking outside the box was required because things kept changing constantly. I had to apply creative thinking to travel challenges.

When I walked into our office at Salerno, my captain asked me how I was able to get back at a time when all the regular flights had been cancelled. I told him nonchalantly that I just hitched a ride with a colonel I knew. He just grinned and patted me on the back. The other military guys in the office just shook their heads and muttered, "A colonel he knew?"

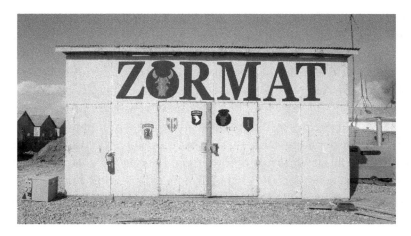

HAVE BUSINESS CARDS, WILL TRAVEL

When the USACE Global unit was being disbanded, the Commanding Officer at Kandahar Air Field (KAF} asked me how I was ever going to get out to my work sites. "No problem, Sir," I assured him. "I know or can find all the right people."

Being a contractor in Afghanistan, I realized early in my travels around my battlefield business world that I needed to be on the minds of the people who could bring me projects. You know the preverbal saying, "Out of Sight, Out of Mind." In a weird sort of way these people were my war zone customers and providers. What better way to promote myself as a valuable resource to these folks than to make sure they had a business card to remember me? Plus, they would also have a way to reach me when needed.

The companies I worked for did not supply us with business cards. I'm sure they wondered who you would hand them out to. Since business printing services were not available in that part of the world, I was left to my own devices. Since I had a computer and printer/copier at my disposal, I figured the best thing to do was create paper business cards.

RMS Readiness Management Support L.C. **Rich Walton** Construction Manager 577th EPBS • FOB Salerno • APO AE Ø9314 Cell: Ø79-813-508Ø • DSN: 318-851-Ø426 E-Mail: richard.t.walton@afghan.swa.army.mil	US Army Corps of Engineers Afghanistan Engineering District -South **Rich Walton** **Construction Control Representative** **PRT ZABUL** **FOB Apache APO AE 09383** **(DSN) 303-551-5655 (Cell-Roshan) 079-747-5251** richard.t.walton@usace.army.mil

Some people would laugh at these makeshift business cards when I handed them out and others would complement me on my ingenuity. Some who laughed decided they needed a way for people to reach them also, but they wanted "more professional" business cards and were going to order them online and have them shipped to them. I never did see any, making me the exception to the rule. And besides, it wasn't just about having the business cards, it was knowing how to distribute them to the right people.

My reality was that my home base moved at a moment's notice. Other than my cell number, my contact information changed on a regular basis so fancy business cards were just a bothersome luxury. I decided to stick with my paper cards, which I could change in a heartbeat and print on any copier.

I couldn't believe I was actually marketing my services in an Afghan war zone. "We're not in Oregon anymore, Mr. Rich," a voice inside me confirmed.

It was way cool seeing the look on people's faces when I handed my business cards to them in these war-torn badlands surroundings.

"You've got to be kidding me," some would say, especially the high-ranking military officers, but, they still took my cards so they would remember who I was and how to contact me when a need would arise. It was not unusual to walk into military offices throughout Afghanistan and see my paper business cards pinned to the wall.

I saw them even in the Romanian army offices. There was Mr. Rich's business card on the wall, with my phone numbers, right next to their mission calendar. With so many military and other organizational units coming in and going out of Afghanistan, contacts were often lost. But for a proactive contractor like me whose contact number was on the wall? Guess who became the go-to guy for design and construction services when a new unit rolled into town? My business cards certainly did the trick. As I saw on the wall behind a colonels' desk, "War is business, and business is good!"

CHAPTER 15

The Rest of the Story

"When we have accepted the worst, we have nothing more to lose. And that automatically means we have everything to gain."

—Dale Carnegie

TOO MANY RAMP CEREMONIES

One of the bases where I spent many months was FOB Salerno in the Khost Province. Because Salerno was a hospital site, they received the wounded and dead soldiers from the surrounding bases. For soldiers who died, there was a special observance called a Ramp Ceremony (some called them a Hero's Farewell) because they were typically conducted at the ramp of the HLC or a C-130 plane ramp. These were the most emotional ceremonies I have ever been to in my life.

Military and civilian personnel lined up on both sides of the street between the hospital and the air field to send the deceased soldier home. A chaplain led the procession with the fallen soldier surrounded by his battle buddies. As the procession comes toward you, as in a stadium wave, each of you salute. After it passes by, you slowly lower your salute, also like a wave. Then after the fallen soldier is loaded onto the aircraft, the chaplain turns to say a few words. Just before he begins to speak, the whole front row of the procession drops to one knee in another wave-like action from the hospital to the aircraft. Once the chaplain is finished, they all stand up.

My first ceremony was mid-afternoon in the hot sun. I walked from my office to the ceremony spot not knowing what to expect. I was hanging back in the crowd, staying behind the soldiers, but somehow kept getting pushed to the front of the crowd until I found myself in the front row among the soldiers. I was so scared I would do something wrong, not being military. Did I salute or I put my hand on my heart? The soldier next to me said "salute" so I did. When it was time, I also had to drop to my knee in the wave. After the chaplain finished, we stood up and all waited in silence while the helicopter flew away.

As the body of the soldier went by, I couldn't stop thinking that there was a mom and dad and maybe a wife and children back home who didn't even know their son, husband, or father was dead yet. I mentally flashed on images of a father back home mowing the lawn and a mother making dinner, just enjoying a normal weekend. Then it hit me hard. Soon they would be notified of their son's death. I kept thinking this could happen to my two sons who were in the Army and Navy. I felt sick to my stomach.

The ramp ceremonies took place at all hours of the day and night as they wanted to get the fallen soldiers home as fast as possible. Even if it was two or three in the morning, we would get up. There were always helicopters patrolling overhead with machine guns ready to lessen the threat of a rocket attack during the ceremony.

One time a helicopter got shot down and both people in it died. I went to the heroes' Ramp Ceremony, having a hard time holding back the tears. My emotions went to their families and I wondered who they had left behind, alone.

The memory of one such ceremony will stay in my mind forever. It was the night a C-130 landed and we lined up behind the plane while the pilot kept the engines running. I stood there in the darkness in one of the two lines formed behind the plane. I could feel the hot prop wash from the C-130. It was not strong enough to knock us over, but strong enough to make us sway back and forth.

From the hospital, the body of the fallen soldier covered with an American flag was carried by several soldier buddies, with the chaplain following them. The chaplain stood on the C-130 ramp facing us and said a few words as always. I couldn't hear his words because of the engine noise. A few Kiowa helicopters flew overhead, ready to engage instantly if the Taliban decided to attack. The ramp went up and the C-130 taxied out to the runway and took off for Bagram Air Field. The night then became deadly quiet and there were a million stars in the sky.

This brave soldier had paid the ultimate price for our freedom. It was really tough trying to hold back the tears. All of us at the ceremony walked back to our rooms. I don't remember anyone saying anything. As I walked, I looked up at the sky and all the stars. I wished people in America could have seen that ceremony. I could only wonder how all of this terrible stuff could be happening. But life goes on. Everyone on the base would get up the next morning and get on with their lives. Sometimes in a bit of a daze, we would get back into our regular routine knowing with all certainty that it will happen again.

PRAISE THE LORD AND PASS THE AMMO

My Grandfather, Isaac Walton, would chant, "Praise the Lord and Pass the Ammo." I understand now it came from a song in WWII. I would think of this every time I went to Chapel.

Back in the States, I went to church on a regular basis and like many other Americans, I probably took the privilege for granted. In fact, I know I did. I believe in God and I enjoy going to church, but going to chapel in a war zone put everything in a whole different light.

There were several times the service was interrupted by the sound of incoming rockets. We sometimes sang a song about the healing rain coming down on us from God. I recall quite vividly how the words of that song made me wonder if rockets would be raining down on us that very same day.

In another song we sang the words, "I praise the Lord in the storm." Back in the states I would have thought about financial problems, illness or family struggles as being the storms to be weathered. But not in Afghanistan. My thoughts always shifted to the "storm of war" and all the death and destruction it brings.

In church at home we prayed for the sick and unfortunate or for a needed boost in life, like getting a new job perhaps. Over there we prayed for a fallen soldier's family who would never see him again.

The chapel was usually full of soldiers with guns. Cell phones were on and being monitored by the soldiers in the pews because of the emergencies that could develop at any time. War doesn't stop just because you are in church. These types of distractions would be unheard of in America and even thought to be rude. In my Afghan world, they were necessary and considered normal. Hearing gunfire and explosions was also unfortunately the norm for the world I now lived in.

Some of the chapels had rifle racks running along the walls next to the pews holding the soldiers' guns. I would laugh to myself thinking you wouldn't see that in American churches, and if you did you'd think these people are pretty radical.

I still recall looking around the chapel and seeing people from all walks of life...folks from America, Korea, Africa, India and many other parts of the world. We had one huge thing in common and that was a shared belief that we are all in God's hands.

Each time I left the chapel, I felt sadness. I remembered having a sense of joy and happiness after church services back in America. Don't get me wrong, I was glad to be able to go to the chapel. It gave me a great way to cope with the trials and tribulations of life in a war zone. I just terribly missed being able to go to church with my family. In my Afghan world, it was a long lonely walk by myself to and from the chapel on Sunday mornings.

As the song goes, "He's got the whole world in his hands, you and me brother." And God does have the whole world in His hands. Being a Christian made living there easier to take, knowing there is life after death.

Typical Base Chapel

PRAYER: THE WAR ZONE COUNTERMEASURE

One day in the Chapel, I picked up on an interesting quote the chaplain used on the days when things were not going well. He shared with us that he says to himself, "Praise Jesus that it is not always this bad." He convinced us that it is all in our minds how we let bad things get to us. The real challenge of being deployed in a war zone is playing a mind game with ourselves. If we let ourselves think depressing thoughts, we will be depressed. If you tell yourself, you're happy, you'll be happy. So, every time I find myself having a shitty day, I just say to myself, "Praise Jesus that it is not always this bad," and I then laugh to myself.

I recall one particular very emotional Memorial Day Sunday service, one that I'll never forget. After opening prayer, the chaplain invited all of us sitting in the pews to stand up and say the name of a fellow soldier who died in combat. He started by calling out the names of some men he knew who had lost their lives in combat. A soldier in the front row stood up and called out another name. He was a little shaken and it was obvious he was choking back a tear as he spoke. Another soldier took his turn. And then another soldier stood up. And then another.

More soldiers kept standing as the names just kept coming out of the soldiers one by one in the chapel. I had a hard time holding it together as name after name was called out. It is one thing to talk about Memorial Day, it is another when the actual names are called out, reminding everyone how real this war was and the sacrifice our military makes on a day to day basis. It had an amazing impact. It was hard to hold back the tears. I couldn't even count the number of days the flags were flown at half-staff at the bases. The sadness was overwhelming.

Going to church each Sunday over there was my way of getting my mental batteries charged for the coming week. By the end of another week filled too full with bad things happening around me, Sunday chapel was the opportunity to get lifted up, dust myself off and start over again.

One Sunday during the summer I was out at a remote base sitting in the chapel tent waiting for the service to begin. The tent was hotter than hell and we were all sweating like crazy. I started thinking about my two sons in the military. Like me, they would be seeing the best and worst of humanity in the war zones where they would be deployed. Each one of us has our own problems and situations to get through and overcome. Many times they would find themselves away and alone, like I was then. I wanted them to know they could find the insight, strength and freedom from these things in God.

TALKING WITH SOLDIERS – LIFE, DEATH, FAMILY

I had plenty of opportunity to talk with soldiers and could tell by the look in their eyes whether they were on duty, just back from R&R, leaving for home, or a "Newbie" just off the plane, first time in a war zone. Many start counting the days until they go home from the moment they set foot on Afghan soil. Some soldiers have family problems while away. Some divorced. It's sad how soldiers are being constantly deployed now. When I was in college, during the Vietnam War, soldiers were deployed once and after that it was volunteer. Now, it seems they are home for a year, just getting things back together and they get deployed again, four, five more times. I believe multiple deployments cause heavy emotional stress on many families.

I now understand how the constant explosions and gunfire that soldiers endure can wear on them, but the frequency of such things actually made them more annoying than anything else, like the constant drip of water.

Many times I walked to my room and thought about how alone each of us was. I was amongst a lot of people. I worked with a lot of people, I went to church with lot of people, ate in a DEFAC with a lot of people, and I worked out in the gym with a lot of people. Yet I still felt alone. I often walked around base only to find soldiers sitting on the steps to their rooms smoking cigarettes looking down at the ground, never smiling. Some look up at me and others don't. They looked sad and worn out. Once in a while I saw a group in the same places talking and only very rarely heard laughter.

One day, two soldiers came and sat down by me at a picnic table. One was talking about watching his newborn son on Skype and how his head was like a "bobble head," flopping all around. I explained that was normal, that his neck muscles were just not strong enough yet. We all laughed as he said it was his first child. I told him, "Just wait till he starts losing all your tools." Then the other guy agreed he did the same with his Dad's tools. We all started telling stories and laughing and for a brief period of time, none of us were alone.

One of the soldiers was getting out of the Army and the other was re-upping because there was still a lot of war to be fought. I thanked them for their service, shook their hands and put my arms around them as one said, "Thank you Sir, and thank you for your service over here." That was the best thing that happened to me over there. We were complete strangers, not knowing each other's names, but I will never forget those words.

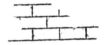

Returning after a Mission

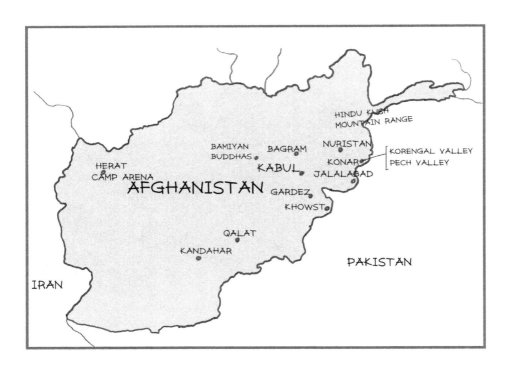

CHAPTER 16

The PRT – Winning the Hearts & Minds

*"A hundred years from now it will not matter what my bank account
was, the sort of house I lived in, or the kind of car I drove ... but the
world may be different because I was important in the life of a child."*

—Forest E Witcraft

When my contract with the U.S. Air Force 577th Expeditionary Group
(Prime Beef) was ending, I was offered the opportunity to join the Provincial
Reconstruction Team (PRT). Being part of the PRT was the best job I ever
had and will probably be the best job of my life. It was a dream job to me.
I was working with both the military and civilian organizations, designing
and building all kinds of projects in remote places. I worked with the local
Afghan contractors and laborers on all kinds of projects "outside the wire,"
which meant being outside the protective walls of a military base or government compound.

I will cherish the memories from that time for the rest of my life. I could
have done the PRT job for the next ten years in complete bliss if it hadn't
closed down.

DREAM JOB - PRT

After the U.S. Military assisted the Afghan people in ousting the Taliban
from power, President Bush promised to help reconstruct Afghanistan. The
PRT organization was established to keep that promise. The PRT was made
up of military personnel, government workers and civilian contractors, set
up to "win the hearts and minds" of the people in Iraq and Afghanistan.

To be able to work for the PRT, candidates like me had to complete five
days of training back in the U.S. in Winchester, Virginia at the USACE (US
Army Corp of Engineers) Deployment Center. This week consisted of briefings on rules and regulations for working as a civilian with the military. We
were schooled in terrorist kidnapping prevention, medical procedures, and
precautionary measures to be taken when encountering explosive devices.
We received military-like uniforms and military identification cards but
were not allowed to carry weapons.

Most PRT projects, I traveled in convoys with other team members in a
group of three to six protective military vehicles to go to the jobsites. Protection

was part of those jobsite travel packages. On some PRT missions, I was able to travel around Afghanistan on my own to all kinds of locations throughout the vast countryside.

A lot of our PRT functions included meeting with regional Governors and Afghan commanders which allowed me to meet and work side by side with an amazing variety of interesting people from all over the world. I worked on places along the Pakistan border, the eastern border of Afghanistan, and also the western side of the country along the Iranian border.

One of the military units I traveled with had a security detail at the U.S. Consulate building in Herat City, near the Iranian border. This was a hotel the State Department had taken over and fortified. It was not too far from the Herat University Women's dorm project, which I was overseeing. On trips to Herat, we would go to the U.S. Consulate first and then to the Women's Dorm construction project before returning to Camp Arena, where I was staying.

The great thing about stopping at the U.S. Consulate was that we got to eat American style breakfasts and lunches in their dining hall. They had great American food for breakfast such as omelets, bacon, ham, pancakes, and hash browns. For lunch they had burgers and French fries and all kinds of other American food. It was a great perk we received as being part of the PRT and I made the best of it every time I got the chance as Camp Arena, where

I was stationed was run by the Italian and Spanish military. That meant all their meals were Spanish and Italian food without much variety or flavor, and we are not talking about Americanized Italian or Spanish food like The Olive Garden.

The humanitarian aspects of the PRT work is what made it particularly enjoyable to me. Helping to build schools out in remote villages was a great reward for me personally. Seeing young children who were willing to walk in their sandals for miles, braving the heat and cold in order to get an education, was a tremendous joy. I remembered what the Afghan Prince in Kabul and I talked about and playing a part in bringing education to those kids made it all worthwhile.

Mr. Rich and Some School Children

I treated all the Afghan workers and soldiers with a great deal of respect, something they were not used to. I worked to help the Afghans better themselves and their station in life at every opportunity. The Afghan people I encountered, whether they worked for me or not, knew that I cared for them and their well-being. They knew in their hearts I was a true friend and benefactor.

In the end, in 2015, I was the last PRT guy to leave Afghanistan – the "last man standing" – and this did not happen by accident. Neither the Afghans nor the senior folks in the PRT wanted me to leave because of the positive impact I had made over there. We built schools, medical clinics, and anything non-military using local workers. The motto of the PRT said it all very well – "Teach – Coach – Mentor." I performed those very activities on a daily basis to help improve the lives of all the Afghans I met. The idea was to give a man a job and a shovel instead of a rifle.

I was glad to stay as long as they let me. The experience was so enjoyable, and I knew I'd miss it.

(Copyright © Jim Ellis used with permission)

ANA KITCHEN – WINNING THE HEARTS AND MINDS

On several occasions, being the only American on an Afghan Army Base (ANA), I would quite often be invited into their kitchens for food and tea. I always laughed and worked at talking with the Afghan soldiers, taking pictures of them and me, then bring printed copies of the pictures back for them on my next visit. They looked forward to me coming back, as they loved those pictures. They always seemed shocked that I would take an interest in them. Did they speak English? No. Did I speak fluent Dari or Pashto? No. It is amazing how you can get by with hand gestures and a smile. I am sure there was the possibility of being kidnapped for a ransom or killed, but for me, this was part of my own "Winning the Hearts and Minds" program.

CHAPTER 17

Working "Outside the Wire"

"Even if you're on the right track, you will get run over if you just sit there."

—Will Rogers

As I settled into my new existence, the reality of my situation could not have been more different than what I had expected. The PRT gave me a great deal more flexibility in setting my own parameters than I would ever have dreamed. Rather than being subjected to a regimented scenario like one would expect with anything related to the military, many choices of what to do and where to go were left up to me. That freedom of choice ended up being somewhere between a blessing and a curse.

My first wake-up call hit me when I found out that with the exception of the infantry, Special Forces, Green Berets and Navy Seals, many of the American military personnel who were deployed to Afghanistan never went outside the walls of the base where they were stationed. Upon arrival, they got off the plane and went to work at their assigned job, whether they were mechanics, computer techs, administrative personnel, etc. A year or so later, they said goodbye to their co-workers and got back on a plane headed for home.

This is by no means meant to diminish the bravery and sacrifice of our troops in Afghanistan, whether inside or outside the wire. Mortar attacks and other artillery strikes did reach inside the walls of military bases and were a serious threat to human lives. It was no picnic by any stretch of the imagination.

Still, I thought it a little odd and scary that I could choose between working inside the perimeter walls of a military base or "outside the wire" amongst the native population. I chose the latter and looking back, I would have it no other way.

Most of the military guys I traveled with wanted me to carry a weapon to protect myself but being a civilian contractor with the type of job I had, I was not allowed to carry a weapon. It was one of those rock and hard spot situations and I was stuck in the middle. I knew I could not change the rule, so I just accepted it and went on with my job.

OUTSIDE THE WIRE AT FOB SMART

One of my favorite work sites was FOB Smart in Zabul Province, where I had many projects during my time in Afghanistan. I got a kick out of teaching the local folks about our building techniques in exchange for learning how the Afghan's built things, but, at the same time I had to stay alert. There had been reports of innocent-looking teenage boys coming up to soldiers, whipping out a knife and stabbing them. I not only had to be mindful of that, but also vigilant about the constant threat of suicide bombers, snipers, IED's and all the other Taliban perils.

FOB Smart was unlike most of the small bases I worked at. It was only about the size of a football field and was located in the middle of Qalat City, surrounded by a wall, buildings and residences. My job was overseeing the design and construction of separate boys' and girls' schools, medical clinics, a radio station and other community projects in the villages.

Building Girls School in Zabul Province – One Brick at a Time

On my first convoy mission, I "dismounted" from the MRAP, and standing in the wide open, I asked the soldier standing with me how much time I had, thinking I needed to be respectful of their time and how long could they be in the open and in harm's way before we had to leave to get back to base, as I was just a guy catching a ride. His response dumbfounded me: "As long as you need sir. We are here for you." I knew my job was necessary for the re-building of Afghanistan, but this was the moment in time when I realized just how important this job was. The only reason these American soldiers were out risking their lives was to protect me so I could do that job.

FROM SHEEP TO KABOBS

I got pretty excited and a bit nostalgic when I was asked to do a site assessment, design and drawings for a new regional stockyard complex in Zabul Province outside the city of Qalat. This project really captured my interest because as a young boy I would ride my bicycle to the stockyards and slaughterhouses to get bull horns to clean and polish, then sell them to my dad's friends. Later, during my college years, I found myself working where my dad had worked his whole life, at the Safeway meat warehouse, unloading quarters of beef off trucks.

After college, I raised cattle, horses and various other livestock on my personal farm back home and definitely was comfortable designing the Afghan stockyard. It felt like a pleasant coincidence to land that assignment. And thrown into the mix was my newly developed skill set of designing buildings using the Afghan traditional mud brick walls and roof systems. Who else over there in the Middle East would have had all these required skills? I guessed I was in the right place at the right time.

I designed and completed the drawings for the stockyards, but unfortunately nothing ever got built due to the lack of available funding.

FOB SMART ATTACK – WORST DAY OF MY LIFE

April 6th of 2013 started out as many of my typical days in Afghanistan did at the time, with a mission out to the Zarghona girl's school to inspect the brick and mortar buildings we were constructing there. I was on the roof of one of the buildings when I heard an explosion. I looked back toward FOB Smart and saw a mushroom cloud. Then came a second explosion.

"Get down on the ground Mr. Walton," I heard a soldier yelling. "We have got to go right now!"

I hurried down the ladder and ran to the MRAP (Mine-Resistant Ambush Protected vehicle). The driver took off like a bat out of hell – crazy fast. Soldiers in the vehicle told me that FOB Smart had been hit. Once we got to Smart, we pulled up to a position in front of the hospital, closing off the street. The gunner on top was aimed in the direction of oncoming traffic.

The ramp and stairs dropped from the MRAP and the soldiers told me to make a run for the base. As I ran down the street, everything I saw seemed to be in eerie black and white tones. I saw several bodies on the ground as I ran to the pedestrian gate of the FOB. Many people were laying on the ground. Others were standing or sitting as if they were frozen in time. Lots of them were bleeding.

As I came around the corner of the first building inside the base, there were more people laying on the ground and others standing but not knowing where to turn. There was blood everywhere. I heard lots of crying. Most civilians were in full-blown panic mode and I saw soldiers who just seemed to be in shock. As I looked around, I saw three bodies covered with blankets. I could not even count the other casualties.

In shock and because of the bulk and weight, I ran to my room to remove my bullet-proof vest and helmet so I could move faster, then ran back to the gate to help the wounded. We started lifting people on stretchers onto the back of a Gator to transport them to the HLZ. MEDVAC choppers were on their way to the HLZ from FOB Apache to evacuate the wounded.

After helping people get bandages on the victims, I ran and got water to give to the wounded. Then I helped get their bullet proof vests and other protective gear off. It was "controlled chaos" – the best way I can describe the gut-wrenching situation. In retrospect, this sounds a little trivial, but I remembered loud and clear the command drilled into us at the U.S. Army Corps of Engineers Deployment Center, "1…2…3…Lift" as we picked each stretcher up from the ground in unison.

Because of the confusion, the only person I remember lifting onto the Gator at the time was a lady from the U.S. State Department. She was semi-conscious and as white as a sheet. All she could manage to say was, "Please don't drop me."

At times like this it is hard to remember what was real versus what I was just imagining. In this case, I do recall a soldier asking me if I thought the lady would make it. I hoped with all my heart that she would. I was deeply saddened when I later learned she died. Several other State Department employees were also wounded in the blasts.

Another very disturbing scene from that day was seeing my favorite soldier friend from the security detail being lifted onto a Gator. The devastating damage his body sustained was horrible, something I'll never forget. I prayed to God to not let my friend end up as a vegetable. My emotions were shredded when I heard he died later that day. I recall him telling me he had always wanted to be in the Army. To me, he was the ultimate American soldier. He was always looking out for me on missions, pointing out what to look out for and where not to walk when on foot patrols. His passing was especially hard on me for many reasons, one of which was because he reminded me in particular of my own sons. I still feel the hollow sorrow as if it were yesterday.

After all the wounded had been transported to the helicopters came the more dismal job of transporting the dead. We would put two bodies on stretchers at a time on the back of the Gator. That terrible day strengthened my bond with the soldiers and I virtually became part of the U.S. military as I participated in those somber tasks.

As I was lifting one stretcher up on the Gator, one of the dead soldiers' arms swung down off the side. It was an incredible effort to choke back the tears as I placed his arm back under the blanket. As we transported the fallen soldiers up to the medic station, I walked behind holding the stretchers to keep them from falling off. A lieutenant colonel came up to help me.

"I can do this, sir," I offered.

"No, I want to do this," he replied. The tremendous compassion in his voice brought another tear to my eye.

I also vividly recall picking up the M4 assault rifles inside the front gate as part of the clean-up. Some of them were melted from the heat of the explosions.

I hoped the worst was over, but then one of my team partners and I were asked to help a sergeant retrieve the severed body remains that had blown over the perimeter wall into the base. We were given gloves and medical bags and told not to tell people what we were doing. Someone did ask and I tried my best to reply as calmly as I could that we were just picking up debris from the blast.

The only thing I could do to help keep it together, was to keep telling myself that I was just picking up elk parts on a hunting trip back in the Pacific Northwest.

I don't remember when, but at some point I had to go retrieve my vest and helmet and put them back on to go outside the base to help. Some U.S. soldiers I didn't recognize went with us for protection as we were tasked to move into the streets to recover bodily remains. As I walked down the street and around a school, there was a smell in the air that I will never forget. It was the smell of death. I had lost track of time by now. All I remember is that it was very hot, I was sweating like crazy and my helmet kept rolling over my eyes every time I bent over to pick something up. I wished I could just take the damn thing off, but there was concern about a secondary attack, and now there were Afghan policemen pointing out body parts for me to pick up.

There must have been children killed because I was picking up what seemed to be the torsos of children and putting them into the bags. As I filled one bag, I would take it to the pedestrian gate and get another. We worked our way to the school soccer field where soldiers had several Afghans in the bleachers and were asking them questions. I couldn't believe how far away the blast had thrown human remains.

Later that day, the news media broadcast the story of the attack. They reported nothing like what had happened. What the shit was that about?

What I learned from several soldiers and was able to piece together, was that an American foot patrol was escorting some U.S. State Department representatives and Afghan officials to deliver donated books to a children's school. The group was approaching the school across the street from our base when a car bomb exploded right in front of them. Then, shortly after the car bomb exploded, explaining the second explosion I heard when I was on top of the Zarghona Girl's School, a suicide bomber ran into the nearby crowd and detonated a second bomb, killing himself and taking a few others with him.

PRIVILEGE CLASS: IN A WAR ZONE

That night following the devastating attack, as we were all sitting in the base dining hall, a guy rushed in and said all U.S. State Department employees should grab a small bag, leave their big stuff behind, and get to the helicopter right away. All the State Department people got up and ran out of the dining hall immediately. A soldier sitting next to me said, "What about you Mr. Walton? You're a civilian."

I laughed, quickly answering, "Are you kidding? The State Department doesn't give a shit about me."

I still had a not-so-fond memory of the time I tried unsuccessfully to get a ride on a State Department helicopter coming back from a remote base which happened to be one of my job sites. While there appeared to be plenty of room on the chopper, I was told there was no room for me. We all nodded our heads in agreement that State Department employees are the privileged class in war zones.

A few weeks later, a memorial was scheduled for the soldiers killed at FOB Smart. When I found out I was not invited to it after all I had done and been through, I was really pissed off. They couldn't find room?

Even though I did not get invited to the memorial, I did get written commendations from a couple high-ranking officers for my actions on the day of the attack. An Air Force colonel said in a letter, "Rich's selfless act of courage bears mentioning. Mr. Walton was instrumental in treating dozens of wounded during a suicide attack at FOB Smart. Rich also volunteered for HR Biologic clean-up that had to be accomplished after the blast, saving some young soldiers the mental trauma they would have endured if they had to perform that gruesome task."

A U.S. Engineer Brigade officer also wrote a letter, saying, "Perhaps the best example of the commitment and dedication of Mr. Walton was his actions during an attack on FOB Smart. Without hesitation, Mr. Walton took action to assist military forces in the treatment and evacuation of casualties during the attack. This heroic and selfless service is a statement to the character, dedication and care that Mr. Walton displays not only in time of crisis but every day, regardless of the situation or circumstance."

Those kind words from senior soldiers made me feel like a comrade in arms and one of their own, which helped offset at least a small bit of the horror of that day.

A couple months later in Kandahar I was sitting at a table and the topic of being shot at while working outside the wire came up. One soldier said to me, "Hey Rich, you were at the FOB Smart attack weren't you? What was it like?"

It was tough holding back the tears as I told them, "Worst experience I've ever had. It smelled like a slaughter house on fire."

I looked around the table and I could see the shock on their faces that I would say something like that. I realized there would be very few people back home that would understand what I really went through and relate to a comment like that. Words simply cannot describe the inner turmoil one experiences after living through such a disaster – the fear, the horror, the sorrow, blurred memories, nightmares – and in the midst of all that, the undeniable adrenaline rush. You want people to understand, but they can't.

A NEAR MISS ON THE WAY TO THE WOMEN'S DORM

The Herat Women's Dormitory at Herat University (Herat, Afghanistan) was one of the most high profile projects in all of Afghanistan and I was glad I had the opportunity to be a part of it. As part of an initiative underway in Afghanistan to aid the education of women in the country, Herat University was constructing a dormitory specifically for female university students.

This was not even close to being the most expensive U.S. project in Afghanistan, but it was by far the most controversial. It marked an important step for women's rights in Afghanistan, and many did not care to take that step.

Afghan women had been denied a basic education under Taliban rule a little more than 12 years earlier, but they were now attending school and college in record numbers. To help accommodate those growing numbers, U.S. Army Corps of Engineers was overseeing construction of the dormitory in cooperation with an Afghan Construction Company. With this dorm, girls from the villages outside of Herat City would have a safe place to live and be able to attend Herat University.

That dormitory was one of my favorite projects in Afghanistan.

As mentioned before, in my belief and opinion, education for everyone in Afghanistan is what is going to turn the country around. Many people question my beliefs on this, but they have not worked side by side with the Afghan people like I have. I blended in with them where I lived and worked. I ate many meals with the local people and went to places most outsiders never see.

The quest to improve the lives of the Afghan people was my main reason for doing what I did over there and the reason I stuck with it for four trying years. I have designed mansions and hotels in America, but nothing gave me more satisfaction than helping the Afghan people.

There were many challenges from local authorities and even from the Afghan police, who were not in favor of this project allowing women to attend college. During one weekend when I was on site, the local police tried to close down the construction by stopping the workers and making them leave the project. The Afghan contractor I was working with courageously confronted the police and stopped them from halting construction. He also solved more confrontations such as "who" had control of this project between the national government or the local government and kept the project moving forward in spite of all the official protests. The contractor persisted even through death threats, eventually even getting arrested and upon release he finished the women's dorm. He and I became good friends during the project as we shared an appreciation for what it would mean to Afghan women and how it would impact the future of the country.

It was not just the Afghans fighting the project that made things interesting. Amidst all the American-backed construction projects going on throughout the country involving many millions of investment dollars, this dormitory project was almost insignificant from a financial standpoint. However, the importance of it from a cultural standpoint was staggering.

Women from areas outside the city of Herat either lacked the financial resources or were culturally intimidated from going to college. Sharia Law not only forbids women from getting an education but may also severely punish them for doing so. This was a women's dorm creating a safe place for females from the villages to live and attend college.

Unfortunately, many families force teenage girls to marry between ages fourteen and eighteen, so they lose the opportunity for high school and college. Without this newly constructed dormitory, those women would continue to be barred from educational opportunities. As a result, the dorm project drew more attention from the American brass, the State Department and other dignitaries than projects 10-20 times its size.

On one particular mission to the women's dorm, we were short one army soldier that particular day, who was supposed to have been our driver. Rather than canceling the mission, one of the engineers and I got permission from the Army captain in charge to drive our own vehicle to the site with the convoy. The engineer and I jumped into a Russian 4-wheel drive vehicle that looked like an old white Toyota 4x4.

I was given a handheld radio for communication with the convoy command vehicle and the engineer drove the vehicle. Falling into line between the Army MRAPs, we drove through the city of Herat. When we got to the women's dorm we found out we had just missed getting hit by an RPG (Rocket-Propelled Grenade) shot from our Taliban friends. It had been just a few minutes after we crossed the Pashtun Bridge on the way to the site when a U.S. State Department vehicle came across the same bridge. The RPG fired at that vehicle went in one window and out the other side but didn't explode until it cleared the vehicle. Unbelievable luck! Dodging the proverbial bullet, the people in the vehicle only got some cuts from the broken glass. I was always amazed at the amount of near-misses we experienced in Afghanistan.

Not long after we arrived, the report of the attack came in and we were ordered to leave the women's dorm and get back to Camp Arena as soon as possible. Base personnel even sent out Italian helicopter gunships to escort us back to the base. While that plan was made with all the right intentions, it did hit a pretty important glitch. I was told by radio that our soldiers and the Italians had no way to communicate between themselves directly. Further, I believe the Italians in the helicopters didn't speak English.

As a show of strength, the Italians flew above and shot some counter-measure flairs over the top of the women's dorm – their version of warning shots. As our convoy made our way back to the base, the same choppers flew beside us. They flew sideways just like I had seen in the movies. It was all pretty exciting. Talk about adrenaline rush.

With no radio communication to the Italian helicopters, I was glad they had not mistaken us for the enemy since even though we were in the middle of the convoy, we were in this old beat up non-military vehicle. We laughed in relief all the way back to the base.

I laughed, "Is this some cool shit or what?"

Fortunately, no one got hurt and I was quite thankful for the Italian helicopter escort. I don't know if that incident qualified as using up one of my nine lives or not, but it sure got my adrenaline going. By the grace of God, we were not at the wrong place at the wrong time on that Pashtun Bridge.

I was unable to attend the dedication ceremony after construction of the women's dorm was completed because the terrorist threat level was exceedingly high. Since I did not get the chance to express my thoughts in a speech at the ceremony, I sent a congratulatory email to all of my contacts involved with the project.

Later, I was ecstatic to be quoted in an article in *Engineering Magazine* saying: "The only way Afghanistan will survive is through education. We're making a difference here by ensuring that the women of Afghanistan can get an education without worrying about interference from the Taliban."

HELICOPTERS MAKE GREAT TARGETS

One day as we were flying on a Russian-made helicopter being used by US-ACE Global into Camp Leatherneck, a stop on our way to FOB Apache, we heard the dreaded rat-tat-tat of machine gun fire. I looked at the British PSD guy at the back of the helicopter and he held up four fingers, meaning four shots had been fired at us. We landed and walked around the helicopter to see if there was any damage. We couldn't see anything so we continued to FOB Apache. Later on, they discovered a bullet stuck in the seam of the outside shell of the helicopter. We were high enough that, although the bullet had enough power to stick in the side seam, it did not have enough power to go through. This was not your everyday commute to the office.

While helicopters themselves make good targets for rockets and sniper fire, sometimes they even made me personally a target. On several bases I visited on my various project missions, the HLZ was outside the perimeter walls of the base, usually because the base didn't have enough space inside its walls.

I felt like a sitting duck whenever I had to walk to or from one of the "outside the walls" landing zones as I was arriving or leaving. Then of course, there was the duration of time, up to three hours I had to wait for the choppers to land. I was almost always just sitting there in the middle of nowhere with no protective barriers whatsoever. I couldn't even count the number of times I sat out in the open at the Fiaz HLZ wondering if there was a sniper across the river taking aim at poor old defenseless Mr. Rich. The military had more important things to do than watch out for crazy civilian contractors wandering around their battlespace.

HELICOPTER TRAVEL – WAR ZONE

Getting to the site by helicopter was an adventure in itself. Kandahar Airfield (KAF) is a NATO base in southern Afghanistan which acts as a hub for all helicopter flights in the south. To get from one base to another, you usually have to change helicopters at KAF.

Being a PRT civilian contractor rather than a uniformed soldier, I was treated as a 2nd class citizen by some KAF personnel. Rather than put up with that crap, I stayed by myself and endured the discomfort of sleeping at the helicopter HLZ in a wooden shack away from the others. It had simple plywood walls with no doors and was furnished with only a few wooden benches and one cot in the middle of the floor.

There was another reason I chose to sleep at the HLZ. To catch flights without a 5-day advance reservation, one had to go on what was called "space available," basically first-come, first-serve standby. People generally started showing up at 3:00 AM to get signed up for the 9:00 AM flights, so changing helicopters over night at KAF was a royal pain in the ass. Sleeping right there at the HLZ meant I was always first in the standby line. It was worth it.

The girls at the counter got to know me and started giving me MREs and bottled water at closing time (4:00 in the afternoon) so I could avoid the rush the following morning. I slept in the unheated shack by myself overnight, reading a book. I did this for months on end – enduring the freezing winter and torrid summer – while on my way to various projects.

THE SHURANDAM RAISIN FACTORY

The first project on which the Army's Regional Contracting Command (RCC) in Kandahar sought my help was the Shurandam Raisin Factory project. This was a $2 million factory compound project that was built with no formal inspections.

I'll never forget my first trip to the raisin factory job site. The helicopter dropped me off outside the wire, very early in the morning, away from the base and then flew away. I was dressed in my military clothes and looked around and said to myself, "What the shit, where's the base?" I saw some Afghans sitting in front of an ice cream plant and roads going in all directions when two Afghan guys on motor scooters came speeding toward me. When I first saw them coming, I panicked because in Qalat where I lived, there had just been several incidents of suicide bombers on scooters. I thought, this is it, just as they weaved on around me and kept going. Even though I didn't know which way to go, I did not want to ask for directions because I figured it might get me kidnapped or killed.

To my left, it looked like there was a green sniper fence on top of a wall a few hundred yards away. I figured it was probably a military base, either American or Afghan Army. So, I walked down the road past more Afghans to a giant steel gate at the front perimeter wall. I started pounding on the gate, feeling sort of like Dorothy knocking on the gate to Oz. It's weird how your imagination runs wild when under stress.

A young American soldier opened a small door inside the larger gate and said, "Can I help you?" Just like *The Wizard of Oz.*

I laughed and said, "Can you help me? What the shit …. I am an American, standing here 'outside the wire' outside your base, in the middle of nowhere, at your front gate! Can I please come in?"

All he could say was, "Sure come on in. Where did you come from, man?"

After I explained that a helicopter had just dropped me off in a field a few hundred yards away, all he said was, "Hmmm, that's weird. They usually send soldiers out to meet people coming in on the helicopters."

I answered, "Oh well, I guess they must have forgot I was coming." This is part of being in a war zone. Shit happens!

When it came time for me to go to inspect the raisin factory, I was escorted by U.S. soldiers on foot back past where I had landed with the helicopter. They took up defensive positions while I inspected the buildings and compound.

I found all kinds of things wrong and missing. No earthquake supports, cracks in the walls, no water. Too dangerous. This is what happens when inspections are skipped. Because of all the construction issues and defects, I

pointed out the facility could never be used as a raisin factory. It could probably only be used for storage with the possibility of the walls falling down.

Shurandam Raisin Factory

After the inspection, the soldiers escorted me back to the base. The next
day, when it came time to leave, I just walked up to the gate and said, "Let
me out please."

They opened the gate and when they didn't offer escort, I didn't ask for
one and I walked down the road to the field, where the helicopter dropped
me off. Afghans walked by and we tried talking to each other. I had my standard US Army multi-cam uniform, helmet, vest, backpack, sleeping bag and
no weapon. I waited alone until the helicopter arrived knowing someone
could shoot me anytime if they wanted.

WHEN THE SHIT HITS THE FAN

We have certainly all heard that familiar phrase, "When the shit hits the fan."
But one day at FOB Sweeney in Southeastern Afghanistan near the Pakistan
border, I got the rare chance to witness it in real life and it was not a pretty
picture.

Just coming back from a walk while taking in the scenery and ponder-
ing my next project, I was topping a hill overlooking the base. I guess my
guardian angel in Heaven was looking down on me that day and probably
influenced me to deviate from the normal path that went past the HLZ and
take a different route.

As I was on the other path about 100 yards away from the HLZ, a chinook helicopter came in for a landing. I could see the chopper was coming in too close to the troops waiting at the staging area.

Sure enough, the prop wash from the helicopter picked up a nearby porta-potty and spun it around in the air, throwing the dung and blue chemical water all over everyone and everything on the HLZ. Wanting to check on the troops to see if everyone was OK, I ran toward the chopper and the crowd of troops.

As I approached, I saw all the brownish-blue water flowing down the pathway. Then I spotted the sergeant in charge of the HLZ, completely covered in shit and blue water, gripping his walkie-talkie with a distinctively grim look on his face. A vision of the Blue Man Group I had seen on a TV ad flashed through my mind, but, instead of him being all blue, there were streaks of brown all over him.

I watched as the troops boarded the helicopter covered with the same blue-brown mixture. The bags they were carrying were covered with the same stuff. Those chopper blades were two massive fans that hit the shit!

Once I realized no one was hurt, I couldn't help but burst out in laughter. I reached for my camera but realized I had not brought it with me. Having just missed a fantastic photo op, I vowed never to forget my camera again. Even though I was still laughing, I couldn't help but feel sorry for those guys and imagining what it would smell like inside that chopper. Then I started laughing even harder as I pictured the faces of whoever would be meeting them at their destination. I could just imagine them saying, "You guys look like you've really been through some shit!"

I looked up toward the heavens and thanked my guardian angel for having guided me away from that HLZ and the "shit storm" that took place up there. I was thinking the folks back home would never believe this one, but you just can't make this stuff up. Only in Afghanistan.

FINALLY, IN A CLASS OF MY OWN

Great ideas didn't always come to fruition. The Army 372nd Engineers battalion contacted me to help them design and build a training Center at the ANA base Camp Hero.

The concept was a great idea because it reminded me of the high school I attended, which was a tech school developed to train students to be tradesmen upon graduation. The Afghan Army wanted to convert an existing structure into a Construction Training Center (CTC) where we would teach ANA soldiers to draw blueprints, frame buildings, and do electrical, plumbing and masonry work. How exciting to be able to design something similar to my school in the US in Afghanistan for the young men there, where I would be one of the key trainers on the faculty. Upon graduation from CTC, these newly trained tradesmen would then go out to the other ANA bases and teach other soldiers to perform the same tasks. Basically, we were to 'train the trainers.'

I began the drawing for the training center renovation as I started to think ahead about teaching my own construction drafting classes. I even started putting together a general outline for teaching the course. I was to have an interpreter for translating my training materials and speaking for me in class. The plan was to have 10-20 soldiers per class. I would be working with Afghan Soldiers that had very little education, so I planned to use visual effects as much as possible.

Some of the young American officers and others laughed at me for planning the curriculum around manual drafting and asked, "Why don't you teach them computer-aided drafting like AutoCAD?"

Realizing most of the young American engineers had never done any architectural drafting without the aid of a computer, the concept seemed foreign to them. I reminded them that Frank Lloyd Wright drew by hand and buildings like the Empire State Building were drawn with pencil and paper.

I guess I was teaching a lost art. I was probably one of the only Americans over there old enough to have created all my drawings by hand. Of course, the Afghan engineering schools in Kabul used computers, but I was not working with engineering students, I was working with Afghan soldiers who were trying to develop into Army Construction Units.

I was even planning to have them make their own tools, such as drawing boards, T-squares and rulers, out of wood. As they made their tools, they would learn how to use them and then could teach others.

I was going to have them draw simple gazebos and furniture like tables and desks and then build what they drew to get a complete understanding of the process of going from paper to material to finished product.

I thought this was going to be a little class with not many people knowing about it, but, it became a big deal when other Afghan Army units found out about it and wanted me to teach their soldiers at other ANA bases also.

Amidst all the mental gyrations of trying to plan my school curriculum, I rolled up my sleeves, sharpened my pencils, loaded all the building dimensions into the Auto-Cad program and got to work on the drawings for the CTC. I produced all the design layouts and the 'as-built' construction blueprints. I felt pretty good that I got all this work done ahead of schedule.

After I had completed all the drawings and was preparing for the next step, I learned the 372nd Engineering unit was being withdrawn from Afghanistan and going back to the States. Just before they left, one of the unit's officers told me the ANA had knocked down the building we were planning to remodel and use for the CTC. Just like that. Gone.

I was instantly reminded of the line from the *Cool Hand Luke* movie when the big fat Southern sheriff put his hands on his hips and issued that famous quote, "I believe what we have here is a failure to communicate."

MR. RICH'S BILLBOARD

On a mission to Herat, I jokingly made the comment to my Afghan engineers that I should have a billboard in the city stating, "I am Mr. Rich, your friend. Don't kill me," so the Taliban would not want to kill me.

One of the Afghan engineers subsequently created a photo of me on a billboard in Afghanistan using Photoshop. He showed it to me and I couldn't believe how good it was. I sent it to several of my friends and they thought it was real. The dummy photo eventually was sent to the USACE headquarters somehow. I had to convince a bunch of the guys there it was not real.

Another promotional material that was created was a poster showing photos from all my travels around Afghanistan of me with Afghan workers and children at construction sites. It was hung in the USACE South headquarters where I was working at the time.

One day, a high ranking military officer visited us at our office for a briefing and happened to see the poster. He was chatting with another officer as he walked down the hall and the subject came up about FOB Walton. "Does this Mr. Rich even have an FOB named after him?" I guess it was a fair question since several bases were named after Americans for one reason or another. I didn't want to explain the whole billboard scam to him, so I just played dumb. My friends started kidding me saying, "Holy crap, Mr. Rich even has a base named after him now!"

Even though they knew the billboard photo was fake, the military guys loved it. It was passed around offices all over Afghanistan. When some of the officers met me, they'd say, "Are you Mr. Rich, the guy on the billboard?"

STUFFED ANIMALS FOR EVERYONE

There were times in Afghanistan when the U.S. Army Civil Affairs office asked me to help them on some of their projects. Being their expert on building design and construction, they used me for both American and Afghan buildings.

One such building was the Department of Women's Affairs (DOWA) building renovation. This project was in Qalat city in Zabul Province in the southeast of Afghanistan near the Pakistan border, and was a shelter for abused Afghan women run by the Afghans. Many of the women also brought their children with them when they came to the shelter. Sometimes I traveled to the site with our troops and sometimes with the Jordanian Military.

After I sent my wife pictures of the children at the shelter, she showed them to our grandchildren. It really saddened them to see children their age with nothing. So my wife asked the grandkids if they would donate their stuffed animals to these unfortunate Afghan children. They sent over 120 stuffed animals in two giant boxes.

The Afghan women at the shelter were so excited when I gave them the toys, they wanted their picture taken with me even though doing so was not really acceptable in their culture.

I guess I could have bought the stuffed animals locally for less than the cost of the postage, but the caring thoughts of my family back home were priceless. When I handed the stuffed animals out to the Afghan children, I took pictures of them to send back home to my family so my grandchildren could see the Afghan children with their stuffed animals they had given up.

Stuffed Animals from Mrs. Rich & the Kids

That following winter I was told one out of four children were dying from the freezing winter temperatures in that area. It made me sick to think about how many of the children to whom I had given the stuffed animals might have died that winter.

One of my favorite photos is of a young Afghan boy who always followed me around when I was at the DOWA site. For some reason, he really took a liking to me. One day when that little boy was sitting down next to me as I took a break, an Army photographer got a great shot of me and my little buddie. That photo is the one on the back cover of this book.

About a year later, I was having a hard time working in Kandahar because of all the static I was getting from some of the USACE employees about not following all their paperwork procedures. In the next email to my wife Shirley, I complained about all the grief I was taking and that it was grinding me down. My wonderfully supportive wife wrote back and reminded me of the stuffed animal episode and other similar incidents I had experienced in many Afghan villages. She told me not to worry about the crap the Corp of Engineers guys were giving me and to just feel proud of the difference I was making with the Afghan people.

"Rich, you are the face of America the Afghans will remember," she wrote.

Every time I looked at that photo of me and that little boy, I thought about Shirley's words and it gave me the strength to move on with renewed optimism. My mind would go into rewind mode just like in a movie, and I would see flash backs of all the grateful smiles I had brought to the faces of many Afghan villagers. A calmness would come over me as I realized I was truly playing a key role in "winning the hearts and minds" of the people.

Unfortunately, around this same time my planned visits to the DOWA site and many other places like it were getting cut short. Many of my missions started getting cancelled due to an increase in terrorist attacks throughout the country and the withdrawal of U.S., NATO and Coalition troops.

In the Qalat area where I was spending most of my time, there was a lot of Taliban terrorist activity going on. Zabul Province, where Qalat is located, was a hot bed for Taliban attacks since it is right on the Pakistan border. We assumed many of the Taliban warriors in Zabul were from Pakistan because they could make a quick retreat to the safe haven of their homeland when things got too dicey for them in Afghanistan. There was an especially heightened danger of convoys being attacked and since many of my missions out to the villages were by convoy, I'd have to lie low for a while.

THE BANK AND AN ATM

One of the strangest projects I was asked to take on involved the construction of a bank building and an ATM in two remote villages. The brigade engineer assigned me the task of going to the two small villages to identify three different possible locations at each village for a bank and ATM machine. At first, I thought they were kidding.

My imagination went wild as I imagined an Afghan version of Butch Cassidy and the Sundance Kid riding into town on camels with AK-47s blazing, robbing the local bank and dragging the ATM machine down the road behind their camels. I came back to reality when they explained the reason for the facility and ATM was so the local ANA soldiers would have a place to get paid and withdraw money.

One of the villages was in a remote area in Zabul Province. I hopped on a chopper, flew up there and met some U.S. Special Forces who would escort me around as I surveyed the village for just the right spots, which needed to be accessible to the local community and the Afghan soldiers.

This would be no easy task so I had to get creative. I figured the building would be a Conex container building brought to the site, so I needed to find a location with water available somehow. I didn't imagine a sewer would be available, so I would have to have some type of outhouses installed. For electricity, I'd either tap into some type of local power source or install some generators. I also figured it should be located near some sort of police or military building for protection. After identifying the three locations, I returned to FOB Apache.

I returned to the village several days later with an Army colonel, showing him my plans. I felt pretty special when the colonel introduced me to the

Afghan Governor of Zabul. He told the Governor I had come from America to help out with projects in his district. They went into a meeting and I sat on the roof with the Navy SEALs who were there to protect the colonel.

They had an old tune from Credence Clearwater Revival playing on their I-pod and that brought back some great memories. I let them know I had seen CCR in concert back in the 1970's.

One of the SEALs gave me a quizzical look and asked, "How old are you?"

When I told him I was 62, he just laughed and commented, "You're older than my dad, man. What the hell are you doing here?"

I just shook my head and said, "Well boys, life doesn't always work out the way you planned."

When the colonel and Governor came out of their meeting, the SEALs cleared the area on the street level so I could take them to the three locations I had selected. Unfortunately, the funding never came through so the banks and ATMs were never built.

So goes the construction business in Afghanistan.

NOT AT ALL LIKE HOME

While I enjoyed the action and challenges, I also didn't mind the austere living conditions. I learned to endure them. I didn't know which weather conditions were worse, the scorching, dusty summers or the freezing winters. How I yearned for the good old days of camping and hunting trips in the Cascade Mountains of the Pacific Northwest. This was pretty shitty by comparison.

And then there were the flies. I was having lunch with some Navy SEALs at a remote outpost once and saw one of the soldiers set a plate of food on an empty table in the corner of the room.

"Who's that for?" I asked.

"Here's a little mealtime lesson for you old man," he joked. "That lonesome plate over there will keep those flies busy for a while and there will be fewer of the little bastards over here bothering us."

It was an ingenious idea. Just eating lunch with those SEALs made me proud to be an American.

I went on hundreds of missions outside the wire with various military units and other security force teams all over Afghanistan. Making travel arrangements for me and some of the people I worked with on projects was one of the things I did as a PRT contractor. I found rides to take me and others wherever we needed to go throughout Afghanistan. I went to all the U.S. military units on Camp Arena and FOB Shindand (an old Russian base, south of Herat City in western Afghanistan) to schedule missions to the US-ACE projects. I also connected with the Italian army units when traveling to sites close to their locations. Another one of my sources was the BSO team (I believe it stood for "Base Security Option"), which was a group of civilian PSD's living off base in a private hotel.

I knew one team from another because of their acronyms and uniforms & patches. There were many times I traveled without the protection of U.S. soldiers. Special Forces Assistance Teams (SFAT) were not always available to get me to the construction jobsites I needed to visit. As a result, I often ended up on missions with coalition force soldiers from Romania, Italy, Lithuania, Jordan or whoever I could talk into giving me a ride to a particular site. It might be the U.S. Corp of Engineers Security Team, Navy Seals, U.S. Special Forces, Afghan National Army personnel or even BSO (an independent private security group). Other groups that I rode with once in a while to get to particular sites were the U.S. Medivac and the U.S. QRF (Quick Reaction Force) helicopters.

What they all had in common was that they all had guns to protect me. A Guardian Angel is a name given to troops who watch over unarmed civilians like myself. I was honored to have them as my guardian angels.

Several of these groups took me to the 'hard to get to sites' that were off the beaten path. Once I was even dropped off in a large open field by a Chinook helicopter and had to hike down to the village through farmers' fields to get to a job site. It was crazy but somehow strangely invigorating.

After talking to an Afghan General about a job site I could not get to, as it was a too dangerous area for an American, he quickly quipped that he would sneak me out to the base by lending me an Afghan Army uniform. I knew this was not an option, but for formalities, I called my Captain back at my home base, who knew me for doing crazy things. On the phone, we could hear my Captain shouting, "Don't you do that. Don't you DARE DO THAT!" Too bad. That would have been another adventure.

WORKING WITH THE ROMANIANS

Of the many international groups I worked with, and one I enjoyed the most, was a team of Romanian soldiers. They always took good care of me, and we became good friends.

One of my favorite places to find missions for construction projects was the Romanian headquarters on FOB Apache. Most of the Romanians there didn't speak English and of course I don't speak Romanian, but it was surprising how well we interacted.

One project I worked on for the Corps of Engineers was the Afghan Ministry of Interior Affairs (MOI) Project, a $6 million ANP compound off Highway 1. I found out the Romanian Army Culvert inspection unit traveled past this site almost daily, so I asked them if I could ride with them once a week and have them drop me off there. I just walked over to a calendar on their office wall, pointed to a day on the calendar, and said "Project MOI" while pointing to myself. I had to get pretty creative in communicating without words during my travels. They understood and were more than happy to do that for me and even assigned a few Romanian soldiers to escort me.

I also had to be very creative to get transportation and protection to my job-sites. When the US Brigade Engineer first found out I was traveling with the Romanians, he said I couldn't do that. I asked him why that was not allowed, since they are coalition partners with us. He checked into it and found out from his superiors that it was fine for me to be traveling with the Romanians. Another small bullet dodged.

On the rides out to my project site, they would practice their English on me, ask me questions about America and try teaching me Romanian. They told me there are two basic regions of Romania, Transylvania and Moldova. I asked the guys from Transylvania if they were vampires and if I had to worry about them biting me. We all had a good laugh about that.

Romanian Soldier – My New Best Friends

The first thing the Romanians did before going out on the mission was to get in a circle and say a prayer. Then the religious leader would put holy water on each man's forehead. On my first ride with them, the leader asked me with gestures and broken English if it was OK for him to put holy water on my forehead.

I showed the leader this was OK and asked him if this was to protect me from the enemy.

"No, it protects us," he said. "Bad things happen if we do not have holy water on everyone."

I fully understood the joke and we all laughed as he administered the water.

Gateguard at MOI

The Romanians smoked a lot in the trucks, which was the only unpleasant aspect of the trips with them. They had Christian crosses hanging inside their MRAP military vehicles and pictures of Saints scotch-taped around the interior, which I thought was a nice touch. In contrast, I thought of how politically incorrect this would be in an American military vehicle. The old saying, "there are no atheists in fox holes," popped into my mind when I saw how religious the Romanians were.

I took great comfort in the Romanian soldiers protecting me from danger even as they seemed so casual walking by my side. In a green on blue attack, an Afghan tower guard killed a U.S. soldier on my base. A Romanian soldier did not hesitate to kill that tower guard.

The female Romanian soldiers were very pretty with their long hair braided or in a ponytail. They reminded me of the Viking warrior princesses and battle maidens I had learned about in history class so many years ago.

I was told a story that when one group of Romanians started checking drainage culverts for bombs, they brought one into an American office on the base, showed it to the people at the desk and asked what they wanted them to do with it. It really freaked out the Americans and they told the Romanians to *VERY CAREFULLY* take the bomb outside of the office.

HITCHING A RIDE WITH THE ITALIAN SOLDIERS

Going on missions with the Italian soldiers was another great experience for me. They always took their responsibility for protecting me very seriously. I guess it wouldn't look good to have an American killed while on their watch. Everywhere we went, they cleared every floor and room before allowing me to enter a building.

I can still hear them shouting, "Mr. Rich, get back to the trucks now!" at the first sign of danger.

One thing about the Italians is that they were consistently late. I always found myself waiting around whenever I was supposed to meet them at a pickup point for a mission. On the bright side, they would almost always bring coffee and pastries for me, so that made up for it.

The Italian Bersaglieri

Helmet Feathers

MY GUARDIAN ANGELS – THE OREGON NATIONAL GUARD

Some of the Oregon National Guard troops from back home got deployed to Camp Arena while I was there, just outside the City of Herat in Western Afghanistan on the Iranian border. Like the other Army guys, they were always willing to take me out on missions to work on my construction projects. It was lots of fun to have guys from my home state out there so we could share stories about life back in the Pacific Northwest. Usually, the first thing they asked me was, "So, Mr. Walton, are you a Duck or a Beaver?"

Having graduated from the University of Oregon, I was a Duck, the school mascot. And of course, the Beaver was the mascot of Oregon State University, our archrival. Most of the guys cheered – obviously fellow Ducks. The Beavers were in the minority and of course they booed.

Besides protecting me, one of the neat things they did was present me with an Oregon National Guard arm patch to wear on my uniform. How cool was that!

THE 82ND AIRBORNE ROCKS

Another fun group that took me out on missions was the U.S. Army's 82nd Airborne Division. When going on missions with the 82nd Airborne, we always prayed first. I asked the Captain how they were able to pray before a mission and other U.S. units could not. His answer: "Because we are the 82nd Airborne." Guess that's all I needed to know.

One of my USA 82nd airborne soldier buddies was born in East Germany. On one particular mission with him, I started to walk into a room before he cleared it. I'm not a small guy, but he grabbed me by the back of my collar, lifted me off the ground and set me down behind him.

"You wanna die today, Mr. Walton?" he said in a thick German accent. He almost sounded like Arnold Schwarzenegger. I assured him that I certainly did not want to die. "Then stay behind me until I clear the room. Got it?" he barked.

I vowed never to make that mistake again. I never felt more protected than when I was with him, and that speaks volumes about his strength and courage since all my other "protectors" were certainly powerhouses themselves. I was both awestruck and humbled by the willingness of these soldiers to risk their lives to protect me. They were all very powerful guys and a lot of fun when the time was right.

Sometimes I would go out on missions without him, while he was off on a different assignment. He would always say to my other US Army guardian angels, "You be sure to watch out for Mr. Walton now. Watching him can be like trying to herd a bunch of cats."

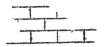

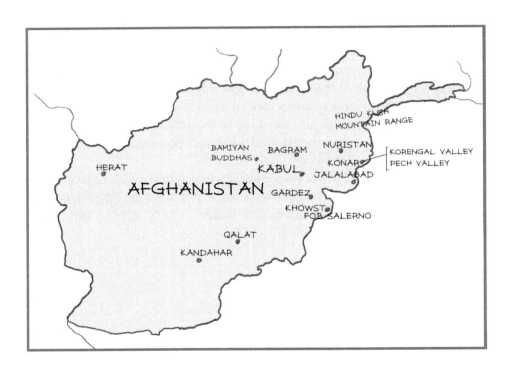

CHAPTER 18

Only in Afghanistan

"When life's problems seem overwhelming, look around and see what other people are coping with. You may consider yourself fortunate."

—Ann Landers

Throughout Afghanistan was the continuous problem of Western standards verses Afghan standards. Construction problems were countless. With the military ripping in and out and Afghan contractors not following the drawings, things didn't always get built right. The Afghans built to their standards and saw nothing wrong with not building what the American engineers required. I was told not to use the term "Afghan Good" anymore as it was not polite and was derogatory. In my opinion, though, that is exactly what they created in their way of building, it was "Afghan Good."

Many bases I visited had septic system problems, generator problems and problems with the Afghans not doing any maintenance or repairs on the bases we had turned over to them. At times I felt like a fireman always putting out fires. Part of the process of dealing with problems was realizing that everyone has problems, so first you had to identify the real problem, face it and then solve it. I believed problems were an opportunity to do things differently and that is what I tried to do working with the Afghans. After centuries of war and destruction, the Afghans desperately wanted to learn. I heard it in their response to my instructions almost every day: "No problem, Mr. Rich."

ROCK-HARD TOILET PAPER

One day I was discussing the construction of latrine buildings that would be used by ANA soldiers with a U.S. government official. He told me he was in charge of a program to teach the ANA soldiers to use toilet paper in the latrines rather than using several stones and bottled or container water like they had been doing all their lives, in outhouses with no plumbing or water. They didn't quite grasp that the placing of stones, plastic bottles and other debris in the toilets was a big problem throughout many military bases.

After his training class, he and his team thought everything would be cool with the new procedure. However, later, the plumbers found out most of the toilets in the latrine were hopelessly clogged with stones. The government official learned that while the Afghan soldiers did in fact use toilet paper after their "class," they were not about to totally change their routine.

The Afghan soldiers had failed to grasp the essence of the toilet training. They still insisted on using stones to wipe with. They thought by wrapping the stones in toilet paper, they would be in compliance. When the stones and toilet paper were flushed down the toilet together...Yes, you get it. Though the US government official couldn't believe his eyes and was frustrated in disbelief, I could not stop laughing. Another "only in Afghanistan."

POO PONDS - WHY ARE WE BUILDING THESE?

We had reports there were problems with the Conex latrines and septic tanks on ANA compounds, so I was asked to do an assessment noting everything wrong with each of the Afghan bases. Shortly after arriving at the first base, the ANA Commander showed up. He had body guards with regular AK-47s, another guard had an RPG and another with a machine gun. Basically, his own little bodyguard army to protect him just like you would see around a warlord in a movie. He immediately told us not to stand in a group because it was too much of a tempting target for Taliban snipers to shoot at. We instantly broke up and spread out.

First, I checked the Latrine building where a rocket had gone through the metal roof and destroyed a couple toilets. It was a simple fix and I couldn't figure out why they had not repaired it. The ANA soldiers were using the toilets on each side of the rocket hole and each time I visited this site I asked why the hole in the roof wasn't repaired. They told me they would get to it. I finally asked them to get me a ladder and I would fix it myself. They refused and assured me they would fix it. This went on all summer and when the snow arrived the hole was still there. The snow was coming through the roof hole and into the building. The ANA soldiers just used the toilets that didn't get snow on them. I soon realized they felt it was either beneath them to fix the hole, or just not their job.

The septic tank for this ANA compound was another problem. I don't know the last time the septic tank was pumped, if ever. It was now a huge sewage pond with plastic bottles and garbage floating in it with mosquitos and flies everywhere, a real breeding ground for disease. Also, it was backed up into the latrines and no one doing anything about it. The putrid smell was everywhere. I saw this situation on other ANA bases I inspected also. It was hard to understand people who would not help themselves and to keep getting the response "it is not my job."

I received word that one of the U.S. women's septic tanks was overflowing. I discovered the tanks to be filled with hard solids and only half or less capacity left in each. I couldn't understand how these solids were accumulating if they were being pumped out on a regular basis, so I decided to check the sewage pump truck. The pump truck had a short hose and could only pump the waste water off the top, leaving the solids in the tank to turn into a hard solid like concrete. The Afghan contractor was getting by only pumping half or a third of the waste out of the tank. The sewage pump truck had to get a longer hose. Thus, Afghan Good.

In several other areas of the same U.S. base, the septic tank capacity was not enough for all the additional people that were being placed on the base. Their solution was to lock the latrines up at night until they were pumped in the morning, so they would not overflow. The soldiers would find an area between buildings to unofficially use for their latrine at night and posted their own homemade signs such as "Piss Alley." These places just reeked of piss, especially when the hot sun came out.

The Afghan Colonel walked me to the conex latrines on his base telling me the Afghan soldiers are hard on buildings. Walking up the steps looking into the conex, I couldn't help laughing. The whole floor of the conex had collapsed and fallen to the ground. This placed the caved-in shower and toilets down about 2 to 3 feet below the floor level on the ground still intact. The Colonel asked me how to fix it. I told him to get a ladder for the soldiers to get down to the showers and toilets. He gave me a big hug as we both laughed at my solution. I did give him a plan to disconnect all the fixtures and pipes and reframe the floor, then to reinstall all the piping and fixtures. He replied, "Who is going to do that?" I suggested if his soldiers could not do this, then he would have to see if there was a local Afghan contractor that could. He replied, "Where do we get the money to pay for this contractor?" Man, this is getting complicated. I just wanted to fix his bathroom.

Neither U.S. troops nor American contractors were allowed to work on Afghan bases and there was apparently little or no money to fix the problems, and the ANA soldiers weren't willing to do it themselves, so nothing got done. Only in Afghanistan could we end up with SHIT everywhere.

ANA GENERATOR PROBLEMS

Septic system failures? Generators were no different. Upon visiting a one-year-old Afghan base with large generators installed by the US, I discovered the generators were no longer working. The generators had either run out of fuel, which the Afghans could not afford to replenish, or they did not replace the oil and the generators burnt up. The Afghans were terrible about doing any maintenance. Almost every base usually had only one very small generator about the size of a lawn mower engine with an electrical extension cord running to the office of the commander as the sole source of electricity for the whole facility.

MORE THAN BURNING THE FOOD

Several Afghan compounds had burnt down their kitchen buildings, mainly burning the roofs as the walls were brick. The walls were scorched and the roof, electrical and plumbing all needed to be replaced. We designed a new wood burning stove design, moving the metal chimneys farther from the roof overhangs that were catching on fire.

WORKING IN AFGHANISTAN – MEDICAL TOLL

Besides the emotional hardship, working in a war zone takes a toll on your body. Nearly all the bases had burning pits where they burned garbage and plastic bottles which produced smoke that was inhaled on a daily basis, plus open sewers and poo ponds. Outside the wire, polluted village water and unsanitary conditions added to the mix.

FLIES IN MY COFFEE

The Afghan Police at the Qalat Police Station expansion loved to treat us Americans great and feed me when I'd visit. One day, they were excited that they had coffee to offer me rather than their regular tea as I arrived. The cup of coffee they gave me had what looked like curdled milk floating on top and two flies stuck in that. The milk could have been curdled because of the lack of refrigeration in Afghanistan. I was sure I'd be sick the next day. There are thousands of flies everywhere and here were two dead ones floating in my coffee they handed me with big smiles of hospitality. On top of that, the rim of the cup was crusty and dirty. Not wanting to offend the Afghan soldier, I picked the flies out and drank the coffee smiling and saying mmmmmm. They walked away happy. The coffee and milk or whatever it was tasted awful and as I was drinking it, I looked at the US soldiers watching me drink as they stood guard. I could feel them saying to themselves, "Mr. Rich, are you really going to drink that?" Yes, I did. The chance of diarrhea was worth winning their hearts and minds. I knew they were offering me the best they had. A few minutes later the Afghan policemen came back and asked me if I wanted more. I politely signaled, no thank you.

When I arrived back at FOB Smart, I mentioned to one of my Afghan interpreters about the coffee and the flies. He told me that was a good thing I had two flies, because one fly is evil and two flies makes it good and that I should have pushed the flies down into the milk and then pulled them out and that would keep me from getting sick. I guess that is an Afghan superstition. I told him I would remember that for next time.

SNAKES, SCORPIONS AND SPIDERS

I received a call from a Security Force Assistance Team (SFAT) asking me to check out the ANA Camp Massoud. Arriving, I discovered the camp in terrible disrepair. Asking why the meal tables were set up outside instead of inside for the soldiers to eat at, they explained they had a problem with scorpions coming in the dining areas, so they ate outside. As we sat to eat inside, I kept looking down at the floor expecting to see scorpions. They asked what to do about the scorpion problem. I had never come across a scorpion problem before and couldn't give any advice on this other than there had to be some locals with a solution. Here again, the Afghan solution to a simple problem was just to eat outside rather than fix it.

As if we didn't have enough to fear being killed by Tommy Taliban, Afghanistan has the world's most dangerous scorpion, the Death Stalker, and one of Asia's deadliest snakes, the Saw Scaled Viper, plus Kurdistan Vipers, Cobras, Kraits, Camel spiders and Black Widow spiders all call this country home. We were reminded of these on posters tacked up in hallways and the latrines. Afghanistan has the types of scorpions that possess the ability to be fatal. The venom of the Krait is 15 times more potent than the Indian cobra. Death can occur in six to eight hours as a result of respiratory failure. While I was there, a Krait was found in a latrine at one FOB and a Kurdistan Viper was found on FOB Warrior, which I traveled through to get to other bases. The Saw Scaled Vipers spotted on some FOBs are considered the most toxic, causing the most severe tissue damage and hemorrhaging. Because food attracts rodents and rodents attract snakes, we were not allowed to eat in living, sleeping and working quarters. Mouse traps were set everywhere.

I was sleeping at FOB Fenty once and woke up with something biting my arm. I smashed it and grabbed a flashlight to see what it was. I couldn't tell what kind of bug it was and didn't know if it was poisonous and there was no one around to ask. I threw it into my boot and hoped I would not die in the night. The next morning, I showed the bug to the military unit and no one knew what it was. They told me to keep an eye on the bite and see if it changed, or if I got sick to let them know. That made me feel weird the next couple of days and nights, wondering if I was going to die. Nothing happened so I guess the bug was not poisonous.

While I was at the same base, a Cobra got caught in a sticky trap and in its upright position dragged the trap across the floor of the building while some guys took pictures and videos of it. As my sons in the military say about their job, something exciting happens every day.

Picking Large Rocks out of Gravel - Only in Afghanistan

CHAPTER 19

Doing Business in a War Zone

"In life you are always selling something, even if it is yourself"

—Dale Carnegie

When I started to do business in Afghanistan, I immediately learned that doing business in a war zone is a whole different ball game than what faces us in the American business world. First of all, there are people that want to kill you for no other reason than to kill you. So you or those around you need to be armed with guns. Kill or be killed is the name of the game; it's that simple. You have no time to negotiate when bullets are coming at you.

UNDERSTANDING LOCAL ISSUES

A Major with the USACE I met while on a PRT project said to me, "In this country where corruption, bribes and payoffs are part of the normal course of doing business, it's not easy to keep critical projects on track." As I worked on more and more projects, I found this to be a stark reality. I learned that aligning myself with local businesses and military contacts and forming alliances with people having access to materials was crucial for completing projects in a war zone.

By knowing their history and culture, I knew if an Afghan's name was preceded with "HAJI", such as Haji Waheen, it meant he had attended the Pilgrimage and successfully completed the HAJJ to Mecca, Saudi Arabia. When cold-calling, upon introduction I'd look the contractor in the eye and say, "Oh, Congratulations! I understand the sacrifice and what you did to complete the HAJJ."

I studied a lot about the Muslim religion and the history of Afghanistan to give me talking points with the Afghan people. I did this for several reasons, and one was to show I took an interest in their religion and culture. I didn't have to embrace their belief system, but simply show them I understood it in order to gain their trust and friendship. This attitude set me apart from the average American working in Afghanistan in their minds. Actually, it's no deep dark secret and I can't take the credit for the idea. It came from my Dale Carnegie studies and the book How to Win Friends and Influence People. Hence, winning the hearts and minds of the Afghan people.

Networking Attire – Afghan Style

There is a vast array of business people in Afghanistan – from college-educated princes, to members of large Afghan corporations, to warlords, and even the Taliban. To work in Afghanistan it is best that you understand the culture, the Muslim religion and the history of Afghanistan. Not only do these things make for better relationships, but they may actually save your life.

Much of what I know about doing business in America doesn't necessarily apply in Afghanistan. When I asked an Afghan job foreman when the concrete would be poured, I might get a reply like, "On Monday, inshallah" meaning that if it didn't happen on Monday, no one would be to blame because it would be God's will. It took me a while to learn how to deal with this attitude, but I soon crafted my own effective reply. "OK, no problem, then you will get paid on Wednesday, inshallah." They would just look at me and laugh. However, the work began to get completed much faster.

BUSINESS NETWORKING – THE ART OF WAR

For me, networking was the backbone supporting the day-to-day efforts to get things done. Networking allowed me to exchange information and services among individuals and the military. I always remembered the four basic rules to live by that I was told by the Afghan businessman: They will lie to you, cheat you, steal from you and possibly kill you. Base all your decisions on these rules and you should get along OK in Afghanistan.

In my opinion, a modern-day version of Sun Tzu's book *The Art of War* should have a chapter added to it entitled "Business Networking in a War Zone". *The Art of War* was written in China around 500BC and is the first known attempt at creating a manual for planning and conducting military operations. I believe that networking is a skill set that must be developed by both military and civilians to get things done in war zones.

There was no textbook for civilians working in a war zone, so I had to figure things out for myself. As I learned being in business for myself for over 30 years, "Rich, only you can make things happen." So I could not just wait around for someone else to do it for me. It was sink or swim. I had to build my own 'Mastermind group' in the war zone environment. My group included military officers, enlisted personnel, convoy schedulers, flight coordinators, material providers, coalition sub-contractors, military construction units and Afghan construction companies.

I knew I had to divide my attentions between humanitarian projects and military projects. I realized I had to be a self-starter and make friends with as many of the soldiers, other civilian contractors and Afghans as I could. I still stay in touch with the many friends and associates I met over there.

I dedicated much time to acting as a sounding board for soldiers, listening attentively as they talked about home, family, their fears and their worries. And when I talk about soldiers, I'm not talking about just the Americans, but all soldiers across the entire coalition. I made it a point to bring treats regularly for the soldiers and Afghan children when I traveled to remote sites.

I was talking with one soldier and he told me I should write a book and call my book "Last Man Standing" because of what all I had been through in my time there and the fact that, with the U.S. troops rotating in and out of the country, I was still in Afghanistan, thus the last man standing. He said, "You have been through more than many deployed military and you are still here."

My job as a civilian contractor in Afghanistan was unique because while I was employed by a number of different organizations during my four and half year stint, I was almost always expected to function as an independent contractor. Toward the end when the U.S. Military started withdrawing from Afghanistan, you had to show you were needed there. In some cases, these organizations did not just hand me assignment after assignment. I was expected to go out and find work projects, which I would then manage and carry to completion. In my position, if I did not find projects to work on, I would be sent back to the States. So in effect, I was an employee, an independent contractor and an entrepreneur all rolled into one, and my business environment was the war zone.

HOW I BECAME THE "GO TO" GUY FOR CONSTRUCTION PROJECTS

By now, you're probably asking yourself, "Rich, what made you so special that the military commands kept choosing you to do work for them?"

Well, in all honesty, I'm not all that special. I was just available. The biggest reason I was available was because I worked hard at making myself available. I had my backpack and sleeping bag ready to go at a moment's notice. No place was too remote or too harsh for me to go to. In addition to making myself available, I worked hard to make sure I was the most valuable at doing the job. Whatever I could do to help the war effort or rebuild, I would do.

I had the flexibility to move around the war zone and was at any commander's beck and call. I quickly gained the experience needed to design things the military troop labor could build themselves with on-hand materials. I went the extra mile to learn how to design structures that could be built according to Afghan methods and materials, such as mud roofs and mud brick walls.

The military commands and other organizations also came to me because I had a "hands on" understanding of Afghan construction methods, culture, history and logistics on how to get around the country on my own. People with things needing to be done chose me because I could do what they needed in a short period of time. I could wade through the red tape and design buildable structures quickly, and then get out to a jobsite in a moment's notice with my creative "hitch hiking."

I also made sure I had access to, or knew how to find, needed construction materials for both military and traditional Afghan applications in the various districts of Afghanistan. I developed a versatility that enabled me to work side-by-side with military workmen or the Afghans to produce the desired results. I was told once by a military officer that every military unit looks for a 'go to' guy that can get things done and I was proud to be that guy in more cases then not.

BUSINESS NETWORK EXPANDS

My relationship with the Lithuanian Special Forces Unit was a prime example of the benefits of networking in Afghanistan. There was a project in Qalat City the RCC was managing that involved an ANA Special Forces compound, and the project was perfect for me. Unfortunately, none of the U.S. Military teams went to that site so I would have no easy way to get to and from the job site. I struck up a conversation with some retired American police officers who had been hired to train Afghan soldiers at this compound. I asked them how they got out there and they told me they had made an arrangement with the Lithuanian Special Forces for transportation when they needed it. I asked them if I could catch a ride with them to and from the site in the future. They said they'd look into it and took my business card with an appreciative grin.

The retired police contractors contacted me a few days later and said it was a go. They told me all I had to do was meet them at the Lithuanian compound when they were scheduled for rides. Traveling with them to that project - I loved it! The Lithuanians were all huge guys with beards and names like Ivan, Igor and such. They came across as very casual, but you knew they would mean serious business whenever the shit hit the fan.

The Lithuanians rode motorcycles. I learned they took their motorcycles on helicopters and flew out into the mountains to hunt down the Taliban on their bikes. How amazing is that? Whenever I would see them riding their motorcycles around the base, we would wave to each other. Good friends to have, I thought.

I found out they liked honey so I had my wife send me a bunch of different flavors from the local farm produce market near our house in Oregon. They really appreciated us going out of our way for them. I always wondered what the guys at the produce market would say if they knew the honey jars they sold my wife were actually gifts for the Lithuanian Special Forces in Afghanistan.

The Lithuanians had a smoking room where they would smoke cigars which had an attached porch and sauna they built themselves. I complemented them on their workmanship. These guys were exciting to be around.

I set-up many missions for myself and for several USACE and other personnel to come to Camp Arena and to FOB Shindand, both in the west, and to

Zabul Province in the east, using them as hubs enabling us to get to job sites in the battlespaces nearby. I did whatever it took to get out to our projects several times a week. When I approached the various coalition units, it was not just about arrangements they could make for me, but also about me helping them with arrangements when they needed to visit U.S. military bases.

I also traded work for transport. One example was when I evaluated a U.S. Army Civil Affairs construction project in exchange for the folks running the project dropping me off at my job sites on the same mission. I also inspected an Afghan Border Guard construction project in exchange for a ride-along to one of my nearby job sites. The only downside of these types of arrangements was that they at times placed me smack dab in the middle of a combat situation with the Taliban.

From my four and a half year experience in Afghanistan, I did get a full appreciation of just how big a part of war business is.

DAY-TO-DAY BUSINESS OPERATIONS

To be effective in Afghanistan, I drew on the skills I developed while running my own architectural design business for several decades back in Oregon. Back in those days, I would remind my employees that while they might think we were in the architectural business, we were really in the service business. And I made sure they understood that the day they forget that was the day we would start going out of business.

A sizeable part of my daily routine in Afghanistan was performing construction duties for all the projects I was working on. To confer with the Afghan contractors working on my projects to review schedules, I would either meet them at the job sites or have them come to the bases where I was living at the time. Projects were virtually always behind schedule. War zones have a way of making that happen, so I was making adjustments continuously.

Perhaps the biggest challenge I faced was getting enough Afghan workers out to the projects. The Taliban was the main culprit causing this, as the workers not only had to fear the occasional sniper fire and rocket attacks but also the prospect of being murdered if the Taliban found out they were working for the Americans.

There were also supply difficulties. Afghan suppliers had no websites where potential buyers could search for the goods they needed, much less get online quotes. There were no vendor directories of any significance. In fact, they didn't even have anything as sophisticated as the old-fashioned telephone book or Yellow Pages we used to rely on in America to find materials and services.

AFGHAN LUMBER YARD (Copyright © Jim Ellis used with permission)
Finding Good Building Materials Took Skill and Determination

In Afghanistan, we had to drive around and find out where we could buy materials and get prices. We could order anything we wanted from Dubai, but that was so expensive and time consuming, it usually was not a viable alternative to sourcing things locally.

Then I had to worry about the materials getting to the job sites. And even when the delivery trucks did manage to get to the site in these remote areas, it was fairly common to find that not all of the materials were on the truck.

"Oh Mr. Rich, some of the materials must have fallen off the truck," was a phrase I heard all too often. Ya, right! Theft was a common problem I had to deal with on a daily basis, or the Taliban stopping the trucks and removing some of the materials.

TERRORISTS MAKE FIERCE BUSINESS COMPETITORS

I had to work amongst Taliban and terrorist sniper fire and mortar rounds. I say both the Taliban and the terrorists because they were not the same. In Afghanistan many terrorists were not necessarily members of the Taliban.

Because of poverty, hunger and lawlessness, the Taliban had armed themselves, first against the Russians and now the current Afghan government. While both Taliban and terrorists claim to have a cause, in reality all they have is desperation, anger, hatred and brutality.

Many people have a mistaken impression that Osama bin Laden was an Afghan, but he was actually from Saudi Arabia. Bin Laden first became involved in the Jihad in Afghanistan when he opened a facility to train recruits, to fight in Afghanistan. Bin Laden was there to fight against the Russians and only after the Russians were driven out did he turn his attention toward America on 9/11.

In my business in America I had to define my market and who my customers were. In Afghanistan my market was in the battlefield and the cost of entry was putting my life on the line.

A WHOLE DIFFERENT BALL GAME

People would often ask me how I could take living like this for over four years straight. My reply is that I pictured in my mind it was like one big elk hunt - camping, living in the mountains, doing without the modern conveniences we're used to in the West. This experience taught me how few material things I really need in life other than food, water and a place to sleep.

I worked virtually seven days a week with no down time. When I wasn't working, there was nothing to do but sleep, but, even trying to get a good night's sleep was difficult. Many nights, I'd lie awake listening to the constant boom of mortars and rockets in the surrounding areas, or close enough to make me get up and run to a concrete bunker, wondering if tonight would be the night the rocket hit me.

Everyday life in Afghanistan seemed twice as hard as it should have been. If I got sick, there was no doctor or drug store to go to. I couldn't just run out and get simple stuff like cough drops or aspirin. If I needed some simple tools like a tape measure, hammer or even nails and screws, I couldn't just jump in the car and go to Home Depot.

Missing my wife, family and friends took a toll on me. The empty feeling of being alone on holidays, birthdays, anniversaries and things of that nature happening a half a world away just plain sucked.

My wife Shirley always supported me during the years I was deployed, which was incredibly important to me and a great comfort. Many soldiers and overseas civilians have huge family issues and some divorce because of the hardships. I met civilians that had just arrived in Afghanistan and had to return home because their wives couldn't stand them being gone. My wife always stayed the course and when asked by others, "Don't you worry about Rich?" her reply was, "I can worry about him or be proud of him. I choose to be proud."

CHAPTER 20

The Final Project – Major General Greene Memorial

"Five great enemies to peace inhabit us: avarice (extreme greed), ambition, envy, anger and pride. If those enemies were to be banished, we should infallibly enjoy perpetual peace."

—Ralph Waldo Emerson

One of the colonels I met and got along with really well contacted me to design a memorial for two-star Major General Harold J. Greene, who was killed in 2014 in Kabul when an Afghan soldier shot him in a green on blue attack. General Greene was the highest-ranking U.S. service member killed on foreign soil during a war since 1972, in the Vietnam War. The memorial was to be built on the NATO base next to the U.S. Embassy in Kabul.

BURNING THE MIDNIGHT OIL – DESIGNING A MEMORIAL PAVILION

When this happened, I was working for USACE and I knew they would not approve the time for me to design this memorial structure as it wasn't one of their projects. I liked my colonel friend and wanted to do my part in honoring the general for his ultimate sacrifice, so I decided I would do the design work at night, on my off-duty time.

I told the colonel it might take a little longer since I could not do the work during the day and he agreed, thanking me for all the off-duty time I'd be putting in. I asked him to send me pictures of the proposed site, which he did right away. He also gave me his impression of how the pavilion would be used both as a memorial and a provisional R&R promenade. Several of my coworkers told me I was stupid to stay up late into the night working on this project for which I was not getting paid. That was the difference of having been self-employed. I knew how to give myself away when needed. I just ignored them because I felt it was an honor to be involved.

I designed a colonnade structure to coincide with and complement the existing tree line already in place. My idea was that it be a comfortable outdoor retreat area for soldiers and civilians to gather and relax under the shade of the trees. It was common knowledge the general had enjoyed going out to this courtyard to chill out and meet with people in a relaxed space.

My design was that of a peaceful garden setting where people could meet to tell their stories to each other, casually joke around, talk about their families, and for a brief moment, escape the rigors of war.

I used lots of wood in the design to soften the harshness of the concrete walkway and adjacent buildings. The finished colonnade has three separate pergolas that provide a minimal sun screen with the option of being covered temporarily when the summer heat requires it. Each pergola area has built-in benches for gathering and talking, relaxing, reading or even smoking. There are also two other areas open to the sky with tables for eating or playing cards.

All in all, it is a place to remember General Greene and the thousands of other American soldiers who died for our country in Afghanistan and to celebrate life.

GENERAL GREENE MEMORIAL DEDICATION

After the Army construction crew finished building the memorial pavilion, I got a call from the colonel asking me to come up to Kabul for the dedication ceremony. I was in the process of finishing up my last three months working out of Kandahar Airfield, after which I'd be returning to the U.S. This would mark the end of my four year stint in Afghanistan and it seemed like the perfect note on which to be leaving. I hopped on a C-130 flight headed for Kabul right away.

After arriving in Kabul, I hitched a ride on a military convoy on its way to the base. Once there, I tracked down the colonel. I walked into the building that housed his office and told them, "Hi, I'm Rich Walton here to see the colonel."

"Hey, Mr. Rich is here," I heard them shouting down the hallway. All of a sudden, people started coming up to me telling me what a great job I did, and that they were glad I could make it to the dedication ceremony. They made me feel really special. It was times like those that made it all worthwhile.

As the colonel gave me a tour of the pavilion, he introduced me to everyone, telling them I was the guy who designed the memorial. I have never had people so happy to see me and shake my hand. It was obvious they knew the story of me going the extra mile to get this done on my own time without pay. I really did not want to take any of the limelight away from the memory of General Greene, and I felt overwhelmed by it all.

They escorted me to a room where I could spend the night. I dropped off my gear and went to the dining hall. I could not believe the spread they had laid out. There was so much food to choose from!

Military brass were everywhere. The tables were covered with white linen and real plates and silverware. I was seated at a table with a bunch of high-ranking officers.

"I can't believe they have real silverware," I joked. "It has been four years since I've eaten with real silverware. Hard to believe."

"So what is it you do?" One of the officers inquired.

"Well it looks like I'm the last PRT guy left here in Afghanistan. And since the PRT work has been winding down, I do design and construction work for small bases and outposts outside the wire in the surrounding provinces."

"Sounds pretty dangerous. What's it like out there?" A young officer asked.

"Not as tough as what the infantry faces every day. It's hot and dusty, mostly primitive."

The next day at the dedication, the colonel introduced me to several U.S. and Italian Generals. I even got to meet the U.S. four-star General Campbell in charge of all Afghanistan, and the U.S. Ambassador, P. Michael McKinley. It was a great ceremony and a great way for me to leave Afghanistan. Everyone was so nice to me and really loved the structure I designed in the general's memory. I was given a General Greene memorial coin and t-shirt. It was really a great honor.

Several days later I was given another coin by a General with USACE for designing that project. I know some people thought this was a USACE Project, when in fact it was a project I did on my own. I then found out there were some people from USACE that didn't even want me going to the dedication ceremony and I had apparently ruffled some feathers. I figured that was their problem. I truly didn't care. Had I not gone, I would have regretted it for the rest of my life.

The USACE General had met with the family of General Greene the week before the dedication and let them know I went the extra mile to do this project on my own time. The General's acknowledgement of my personal contribution to the memorial added to the feeling that I had truly made a difference over there.

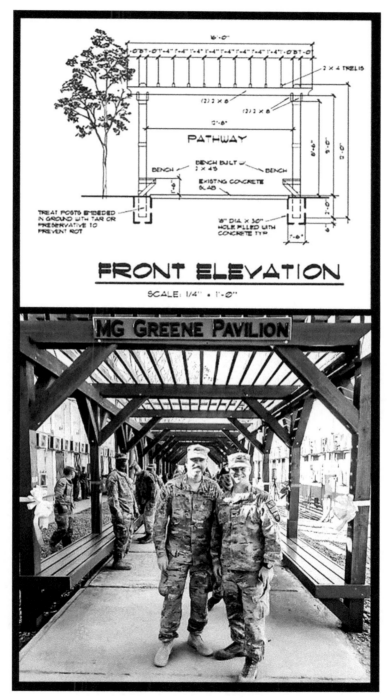

My Drawing and The Colonel & I

CHAPTER 21

Afghanistan in My Rear-View Mirror

Trying to explain deployment to a war zone, is like trying to explain the taste of salt to someone who has never tasted salt.

—Rich Walton

When I started my four-and-a-half-year journey to Afghanistan as a naïve American civilian contractor, I knew next to nothing about the military and war. Those years of experiences in Afghanistan transformed me into a hardened and more callous person, unafraid of death.

I swear more than I used to and have less tolerance for those that mean to do us Americans harm. I wondered how I was going to be able to experience the adrenaline rush back home that I became used to on missions in Afghanistan. I realized this is the same situation our American soldiers must face.

Perhaps the biggest change in me is my view of life. Living a life deprived of the comforts of home made me realize how little I really needed many of the things I used to consider necessities. I am now much happier with my station in life in spite of the fact that I no longer have my own architectural design company I enjoyed for so many years. I am content with a much simpler lifestyle now.

Another big change I never anticipated was losing my fear of death. While I have always been a person with strong religious faith, thoughts of "feasting on lamb in Paradise" have given me a more neutral perspective on death. When it happens, it happens, and Mr. Rich has no problem with that. I have made my peace with God and I'm good to go.

I miss the enjoyable conversations I used to have with many of the Afghan friends and business people I met over there. In spite of significant cultural and religious differences, I developed some really good friendships during my four-year adventure. A sense of brotherhood formed and we all looked forward to the day of no war and to the prosperous rebuilding of Afghanistan through the education of its children and young people.

Once I had settled into my new-found Afghan adventure, I realized how much I loved to talk about history. I sought out conversations that would give me more insights into the history of that part of the world. I had studied a lot of world history in my life and I found this a big help in making conversations more interesting. And it was not just conversation with the Afghans themselves. My Lebanese friends and many U.S. Soldiers loved what I had to share. I would chat with whomever would listen. The Afghan people were surprised that I knew so much about their country's history and religion and loved to talk to me about it.

I thank God my job outside the wire gave me the opportunity to spend quality time with Afghan people. There is no way this could have happened had I lived on a secure military base. Was I putting my life in danger? Yes. But there are some things in life worth the risk. My interest in the country's culture and history really solidified the Afghans' trust in me. At those times when I was stuck on a big base, I would find myself yearning to get back outside the wire with the local people.

CONFESSIONS OF AN ADRENALINE JUNKIE

As I was preparing to wrap up my final jobs and leave Afghanistan, my emotions were surprisingly mixed. On the one hand, I was so happy to be going home to be with my wife and family. On the other, I knew I would miss the feeling of being needed, the continuity I brought to both the Afghans and the U.S. Military. Also, I would miss the friendships I had formed, and the good times those relationships brought me along with the thrill of the rush of life I had become accustomed to.

As warped as it sounds, there was a darker side to what I'd be missing. How dull everyday life would be without the thrill of danger. How was I ever going to get this type of excitement back in America? Accepting the thought of death being something other than a bad thing is only the tip of the iceberg. My thought process has changed dramatically since my Afghanistan adventure. As much as I hate to admit it, the thought of *not* living in danger seems a little boring. I feel like a moth drawn to a flame sometimes. I know it can harm me, but it's like I can't help myself.

The thrill and excitement of working outside the wire in a war zone is something I just can't put into words. I'll admit it: I'm a little crazy. During my four year stint in the Afghan war zone, I met many soldiers from several countries. I was surprised at the large percentage of those who had an even more advanced adrenaline addiction than I had developed. Needless to say, it made for some very enlightening conversations. One of the side effects of the adrenaline rush is that, when it is over, the mind starts to wander. You think of bullets you've dodged, bombs that missed you, and why others were killed and you weren't.

I also recall the many meaningful conversations I had with young soldiers who were definitely not over there for the thrill of death-defying experiences. I talked with a lot of these young guys and gals while waiting to get on a chopper with them. I'd always ask where they were from. The guys would tell me about their wives or ex-wives and children back home. I tried giving them as much moral support as I could by taking the time to listen. I realized how hard it was on them and their families, and I made sure I thanked them for their service.

LESSONS LEARNED

While I was only in Afghanistan for just over four years, the U.S. was involved in warfare over there for 13 years (2001-2014). That sounds like a long enough time to win the war, especially when we were not there alone, but with Coalition and NATO Forces. Think about that for a minute. Given the constant military turnover, most military tours of duty run from nine to eighteen months. Each 'shift change' of the military virtually started over from scratch. In my four years, I saw the same learning curve repeated again and again. In my own view, it's not really like the US, Coalition and NATO Forces had been there for 13 years. It's more like we'd been there for one year, and just repeated it 13 times.

I wish people in America would realize nothing is off limits to terrorists. Placing bombs on women and children is nothing to them. The end justifies the means in their mind. We in the West just can't imagine strapping a bomb on a child and using him to blow people up. It is this type of naïveté the terrorists depend on.

The U.S. Army Corp of Engineers and others like them are great organizations but are too big and bureaucratic to operate effectively in a war-torn country. Don't get me wrong, I have a great deal of respect for the USACE and I made many friends throughout that organization.

This is just my opinion, but I believe what is needed is a small force to take on small austere projects that often call for quick solutions developed and implemented on the fly. Move in fast, get the job done and get out and on to the next job. Speed and utility should override the enforcement of strict building standards when needed on a case by case basis. For lack of a better term, it would be a 'design and build as you go' scenario.

PEASE GREETERS – RETURNING HOME

One of the most moving and unforgettable events of my tour in Afghanistan was coming home through the Pease Airport at Portsmouth, New Hampshire. I went through this facility two of the times that I returned to the USA.

Arriving with military troops returning home from deployment on the Freedom flight from Kuwait, we were greeted by the local town with food and drinks, free phone calls available, warm cheers and gratitude, and lots of hugs from volunteers welcoming us back to the USA and thanking us for our service. My first flight arrived at 2:00 am with snow outside, but it appeared the whole town showed up, young and old, no matter what time it was. It was so unexpected, I choked up, so proud to be American. The second time through, I arrived in the afternoon. I was surprisingly greeted by many of the same people who recognized me, as I stood out as an older civilian with a beard. They have done this for over 1000 flights.

Every time flights arrive they take a group photo and hang it up on the wall of the airport and give each of us a hand knitted hat and an embroidered star cut from a retired American flag with a note: "I am a part of our American flag. I have flown over a home in the USA. I can no longer fly, the sun and winds have caused me to become tattered and torn. Please carry me as a reminder that you are not forgotten."

It was fun to see my first time flight picture on the wall when I went back through. The patriotism of the people of the state of New Hampshire is well expressed in their State Motto: "Live Free or Die."

SHALL I RETURN?

I was in college during the Vietnam War, when the U.S. had the first lottery to be drafted into the Army and my draft number was 74. At that time anybody below 125 was drafted, but I had a student deferment and by the time I graduated, the war was over and our military was downsizing. In later years I was haunted by not joining the military and doing "my part."

Since my return to the United States from Afghanistan, I've had many lengthy discussions with relatives, friends and business associates about my experiences. The question that invariably comes up is this: "Rich, will you ever go back and do something like that again?"

I Miss Working With These Guys

I've done lots of soul-searching as I've tried to find an answer to this question. I didn't set out to do anything. It just happened. I felt it was my big second chance in life to prove who I really am and what I have to offer. It was all that and more. It was great to be able to have such a positive impact on both the Afghan citizens and U.S. military soldiers. It's obvious from all the feedback I got that I touched many of the Afghans in ways they never thought possible. I became their friend and they became mine.

The guilt I had carried for so many years about not "doing my part" is gone forever. I now feel I have served my country with distinction and I feel proud about that. I can look my friends and family members who have chosen to do their military duty in the eye and proudly say, "I have been there and I have done that."

For the rest of my life I will be looking for the opportunity to get back into the fight in defending our country, helping the military any way I can and working with the local people. I'd much rather die of a rocket blast in a war zone than waste away in a nursing home.

Many people never find their dream job. I was lucky enough to find mine and that job was working for the PRT in Afghanistan. I feel I was actually a part of history in the making and that I was needed in the lives of people and communities, making a difference in "winning the hearts and minds" of the Afghan people.

What they don't know is **they also won my heart and mind.**

For more Stories, visit www.OneBrickataTimePress.com

Always Nice to Be Appreciated

In writing this book, I never realized how much soul searching and agonizing I would have in trying to put my stories and experiences in written form.

Aside from the pleasure I got from dodging bullets from Taliban snipers, one of the positive elements of the work I was doing for the various commands and organizations in Afghanistan was the commendations I received for a job well done. It's always rewarding to see in writing how much my efforts meant to other people.

Here are a few random samples:

U.S. Army Corp of Engineers (USACE)

"Mr. Walton was my chief USACE engineer at FOB Smart, Zabul Province, Afghanistan from Oct 2012 - June 2013. During that time, he provided superior service to me as the PRT Commander and the men and women that he served with. Rich was able to successfully complete all 11 high profile CERP projects that we assigned to him. He did it all on or ahead of schedule and under budget."

—Lt Col USAF

U.S. Army Civilian Affairs RTTC (Regional Teacher's Training College)

"I have worked with Rich on several construction projects. He has demonstrated superior engineering and contract skills in dealing with difficult construction problems."

—Acquisition Analyst Principal Regional Contracting Center

USACE/CERP University of Herat Women's Dorm

"While working with Mr. Rich Walton, we realized his warm feelings, kindness, and concerns towards the people of Afghanistan. We also learned a great deal about many technical matters concerning the construction of our project."

—Abdullah Foushanji, CEO, Poushang Construction Company

Military Acronym and Terminology

ABP - Afghan Border Patrol

ANA - Afghanistan National Army

ASG - Afghan Security Guard

Battlespace – A geographically defined area controlled by a specific military base. Also called an AO (Area of Operation).

BAF – Bagram Airfield.

CERP - **Commander's Emergency Response Program** – A money fund for military commanders to use for conducting rebuilding and reconstruction during the Iraq and Afghanistan Wars.

Conex – Also called Conex box - A large metal cargo container used primarily for shipping supplies.

COP - Combat Outpost. A small base which can contain between 40 and 150 service members and is usually placed in hostile locations.

DFAC - Dining Facility.

DoD – U.S. Department of Defense

FOB - Forward Operating Base. A base that is larger than a COP (command Outpost), but smaller than a super-base

Green on Blue attack – An attack on a member of one coalition military by a member of an Afghan military or police unit

Guardian Angel - A soldier placed in a high position in urban warfare to watch over friendly units and/or civilians.

HLZ - Helicopter Landing Zone - A specified ground area for landing both military and civilian helicopters.

IED - Improvised Explosive Device. A home-made bomb.

ISAF - International Security Assistance Force.

JBAD – Jalalabad Air Field/ Fob Fenty.

KAF – Kandahar Airfield.

Latrine – Bathroom, Potty

M4 - The M4 carbine is a military grade assault rifle that replaced the M16 rifle in most Army and Marine Corps combat units as the primary infantry weapon.

MRAP - Mine-Resistant Ambush Protected - a United States military term for vehicles that are designed to withstand improvised explosive device (IED) attacks and ambushes.

MRE – Meal Ready to Eat. A 3,600 calorie meal packaged in a wrapper.

OP – Observation Post – A very small base, usually on top of a mountain, giving oversight for nearby bases.

Outside the Wire – Refers to the area outside the perimeter walls of a military base.

PRT - Provincial Reconstruction Team. Made up of military and civilian personnel to win the hearts and minds of the people in Iraq and Afghanistan.

PX – Post Exchange – A store on a military base offering groceries, sundries, etc.

RCC – Regional Contracting Centers - the U.S. military relies on Regional Contracting Centers to work with Afghan businesses and contractors to provide goods and services for military installations and construction projects throughout the country.

RPG - Rocket-Propelled Grenade, a shoulder-fired, anti-tank weapon system that fires rockets equipped with an explosive warhead.

SFAT - Security Force Assistance Team.

TOC - Tactical Operations Center – A small command center for military operations.

USACE - U.S. Army Corps of Engineers

USAID - United States Agency for International Development

Study Questions
For Book Clubs and Individuals

1. What do you think Mr. Rich's point and reason is for writing this book?

2. After Mr. Rich lives through the car bomb explosion in Kabul how did that change Mr. Rich's outlook on life?

3. What do you think the businessman was trying to get across to Mr. Rich when he told him to remember these four things to survive in Afghanistan. "We Afghans will lie, cheat, steal and try to kill you. Base all your decisions on these principles and you should do fine."

4. What is the significance of the irony in the story of the man killing his neighbor and then giving his daughters to the men of the murdered man's tribe?

   How is this type of justice different from American justice?

5. Compare the different living and safety conditions between the two larger bases of Bagram and Kandahar and the smaller remote bases.

   How did the rules vary such as drinking alcohol for the US State Department personal and US Military soldiers? Was that fair?

6. Mr. Rich was quoted in an engineering magazine to say "the only way Afghanistan will survive is through education". What does this mean and why is this so important?

7. How did Mr. Rich's knowledge of Afghanistan history help him in Afghanistan?

   How did his knowledge of the Quran and Muslim religion help him?

8. How do you think the FOB Smart attack and what Mr. Rich did changed how the military felt about him?

9. What do you think the difference is on how the war is perceived between those on the larger bases and those on the smaller remote bases?

10. Why is it so important to have continuity between military units coming in and going out of Afghanistan?

11. How would you work, build structures and communicate with people who cannot read or write?

12. What is an Adrenaline Rush in a war zone and why is that important?

   Can that become addictive and harmful to one's health?

13. Is there any importance to having U.S. civilians working in a war zone?

   How is this both a negative and positive relationship?

14. Why is it important to educate girls in Afghanistan?

   What more can be done to educate a higher number of girls?

15. Why are pencils & pens so important to Afghan children?

16. Mr. Rich witnessed his immediate surroundings change dramatically from the safety of living in America to war zone in Afghanistan within a short period of time.

   How does he respond to these changes?

Resources

Additional books you might enjoy
about the military and time of war

1. *American Sniper: The Autobiography of the most Lethal Sniper,* by Chris Kyle with Scott McEwen and Jim DeFelice. William Morrow and Company, 2012

2. *Be Safe, Love Mom: A military mom's stories of courage and surviving life on the home front,* by Elaine Brye with Nan Gatewood Satter. Perseus Book Group, 2015

3. *Charlie Wilson War,* by George Crile. Atlantic Monthly Press, 2007

4. *Civilian Warriors: The Inside story of Blackwater and the Unsung Heroes of the War on Terror,* by Erik Prince. Portfolio / Penguin Group, 2014

5. *Horse Soldiers,* by Doug Stanton. Scribner / A Division of Simon & Schuster, Inc, 2009

6. *I am Malala,* by Malala Yousafzai with Christina Lamb. Back Bay Books / Little Brown and Company, 2013

7. *In the Graveyard of Empires: America's War in Afghanistan,* by Seth G. Jones. W.W. Norton & Company, 2010

8. *Into the Fire: A Firsthand account of the most extraordinary battle in the Afghan War,* By Dakota Meyer with Bing West, Random House Trade, 2013

9. *Kabul Beauty School,* by Deborah Rodriguez/Kristin Chison. Random House, 2007

10. *Lone Survivor,* by Marcus Luttrell with Patrick Robinson. Back Bay Books /Little, Brown and Company, 2007

11. *The Good Soldier,* by David Finkel. Picador / Sarah Crichton Books / Farrar, Straus and Giroux, 2009

12. *The Kite Runner*, by Khaled Hosseini. Riverhead Books an imprint of Penguin Random House LLC, 2013

13. *The Unforgiving Minute*, by Craig M. Mullaney. Penguin Group, 2009

14. *Three Cups of Tea*, by Greg Mortenson and David Oliver Relin. Penguin Books, 2007

15. *War*, by Sebastian Junger. Twelve, 2007

16. *What it is like to go to War*, by Karl Marlantes. New York: Atlantic Monthly Press, 2011

A Few Military Bases with Memorials in Afghanistan

FOB SMART in Qalat

THIS PRT. QALAT AFGHANISTAN
IS DEDICATED TO

LTC ALBERT E. SMART

422ST CIVIL AFFAIRS BDE
SAN ANTONIO, TEXAS

A PROFESIONAL SOLDIER
DEDICATED FATHER AND
INSPIRATIONAL LEADER

WE WILL NEVER FORGET

2003-2004 OEF IV

FOB LAGMAN in Zabul Province, Qalat

THE PECH RIVER VALLEY in Konar

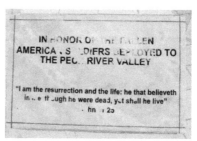

IN HONOR OF THE FALLEN
AMERICAN SOLDIERS DEPLOYED TO
THE PECH RIVER VALLEY

"I am the resurrection and the life: he that believeth
in me though he were dead, yet shall he live"
- John 11:25

< 223 >

FOB BORIS in Paktika Province

FOB SHARANA in Sharana

OUTPOST MONTI in Konar

FOB SWEENEY in Shinkay

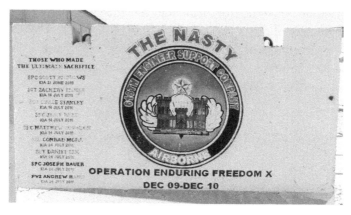

About The Author

Rich Walton had his own Architectural Design business for 30 years, winning several awards for his home designs in the Pacific Northwest. Upon accepting work in Afghanistan in 2009, Rich soon gained a passion for winning the hearts and minds of the Afghan people in remote areas by helping build schools that made education available to boys and girls. He firmly believes the only way Afghanistan will survive is through education.

Walton worked in Afghanistan for over four years, traveling all over the country as a construction manager and architectural designer, helping build facilities for both the U.S. and Afghan armies. More importantly, Rich was a key member of the Provincial Reconstruction Team (PRT), where he designed and helped construct medical facilities, the Herat University women's dorm, and a variety of other projects.

Walton is a graduate of the University of Oregon and along with his wife, Shirley, was co-president of the United States Naval Academy Parents Club of Oregon & Southwest Washington.

About The Speaker

Upon the return from 4.5 years of service as an American Construction Contractor in Afghanistan Rich Walton has had the unexpected and many times unplanned opportunity to speak about his experiences with the people, in the places and the work completed there.

Rich shares his passion through storytelling with humor plus the seriousness and concern for Afghanistan and its people. Many stories make his audiences laugh while others bring tears. The subject matter and the stories shared are age-appropriate and with keen sensitivity for the individual groups.

Rich gives talks, keynote addresses, workshops for the following groups.

Veteran groups – Church Groups – Schools – Teachers and Children Business Groups - Civil Groups – Civic Groups

His topics include:

- **History in the Making**

  The military situation and the Afghan people then and now.

- **Rebuilding Afghanistan One Brick at a Time**

  The culture, religion and what it was like living in Afghanistan and Rich's work as an American Contractor

- **Battle for the Hearts & Minds**

  Stories about the children and schools Rich helped build. What a prized possession just a pencil is to children in Afghanistan.

- **Education & Culture under the Taliban**

  Firsthand experiences and understanding about the culture validating a better understanding to students reading the book "*I am Malala*".

- **Between Businessman & Taliban**

  How Networking was a major part of daily routine - even in a Third World War Zone Environment.

- **The Face of America Afghans will Remember**

  The interrelationship Rich experienced with the military, political, social, cultural, Education.

For more information about Rich and his experiences or to invite him to your group

Go to **www.OneBrickataTimePress.com** or contact **Speaker@OneBrickata-TimePress.com**

To read the Conversations with Mr. Rich go to **www.OneBrickataTimePress.com/Mediaroom**

CPSIA information can be obtained
at www.ICGtesting.com
Printed in the USA
BVHW041920090322
631071BV00013B/560